The Adirondack M

CANOE GU
WESTERN AND CENTRAL NEW YORK STATE

Mark W. Freeman, Series Editor

Alice Broberg and Daan Zwick, Regional Coordinators

First Edition

The Adirondack Mountain Club, Inc
Lake George, NY

Rivers are forever changing; neither the editor nor ADK and its contributors assume responsibility for inaccuracies in this book or for the safety of people on the rivers.

Library of Congress Cataloging-in-Publication Data

The Adirondack Mountain Club Canoe Guide to Western and Central New York State / edited by Mark Freeman.—1st ed.
p. cm. —(The Adirondack Mountain Club Canoe Guide series; v.1)

Includes index.
ISBN 0-935272-59-3

1. Canoes and canoeing—New York (State)—Guidebooks. 2. New York (State)—Guidebooks. I. Freeman, Mark 1927– II. Adirondack Mountain Club. III. Series.

GV776.N7A35 1993
797.1'22'09747—dc20 93-25704
CIP

Design and cover photograph by Allison W. Bell
Printed and bound in the USA

Table of Contents

• • • • WESTERN & CENTRAL NEW YORK

Part IV: LAKE ONTARIO DRAINAGE, WESTERN PART

Part V: LAKE ONTARIO DRAINAGE, EASTERN PART

• • • • WESTERN & CENTRAL NEW YORK

"There is nothing—absolutely nothing—half so much worth doing as simply messing about in boats . . . In or out of 'em, it doesn't matter."

—*The Wind in the Willows,* by Kenneth Grahame

This book is dedicated to my wife, Anne,
my constant joy and support, in and out of boats,
for the past forty-seven years.

What This Guide Is Not

This guide is not a treatise on how to paddle. It does not discuss the relative merits of various craft, nor attempt to persuade the reader that canoeing is a good way to spend his time. It is not a course in geology, botany, or zoölogy. It is not an ode to rivers.

The assumption of the editor is that most people who buy canoe guides know how to paddle, more or less; that they own a boat or know where they can get one; and that they are already hooked on canoeing. If they're not, they soon will be. What the buyer wants from a guidebook is a clear, simple, and above all, accurate description of the canoe trip to be taken. To the degree that it is humanly possible, this book provides that.

Introduction

Every entry in this book was provided by an experienced canoeist who was on the scene. Then it was checked and rechecked. Anyone who uses a canoe guide must realize that obstacles like trees and barbed wire fences may change tomorrow. Even boulders can move; dams can be torn out or built. Legal access areas can become posted private property and vice versa. Perhaps most important, a stream that is a kitten at M water level can be a sabertooth tiger when it is in flood. No book is a substitute for common sense, good river judgment, sufficient skill for the challenge, and looking ahead from time to time, even if that means pulling over to the bank and getting out and walking in order to see around the next corner.

Canoeing is unique among sports in that it can be as Spartan or sybaritic as the practitioner desires. There are trips in this guide which describe an uphill carry of five miles, or sliding canoe, gear, and paddlers down a steep rocky slope; there are trips through flat marshes filled with carp and cranes. The canoeist can camp out in the wilderness with only the supplies he carried in, or make all portages by car and sleep in a luxurious motel every night.

No other sport is like canoeing in another regard: one moment a party is paddling down a river, laughing and talking; the next moment someone is in the water, being swept downstream, rapidly getting chilled, and terrified. We have all experienced it; the danger is as real as the fun. If canoeing, especially whitewater canoeing, were as dangerous as some people think, races like the annual one on the Hudson at North Creek would not have been held for over twenty years without a single fatality. Nonetheless, the sport can result in experiences that are both terrifying and life threatening. Furthermore, a spill into a relatively warm and slow-moving river in July can be a joke, while a spill at the same location in April can kill you very quickly.

The chief risks in canoeing are drowning, hypothermia, and injury from collision with an obstacle, including another boat. The canoeist's chief protections from these unpleasant happenings include the necessary skills and equipment, the moral courage not to tackle streams he's not sure he can handle, and good common sense. The only other defense is to stay home and plant petunias in the boat.

Proper garments include a personal flotation device (what you and I call a life jacket), sufficient, layered warm clothing, a wet suit and/or a helmet if the situation warrants, and correct footwear. Most of the time, sneakers designed for wading, either originally by their manufacturer or subsequently by their owner, will suffice. Bare feet are not best for canoeing, nor bare bodies. Aside from cold, sunburn, while not life-threatening, can be serious. The canoeist should be constantly asking himself, "If I fall in this river in the next five minutes, am I dressed properly for the occasion? How will I get out? How will my companions help me?"

A person in water under 50° F., without a wet suit, has at best a few minutes to do something about his condition before it deteriorates to the point at which he is no longer capable of helping himself. Disorientation and loss of judgment are very quickly brought on by hypothermia. An accepted rule of thumb is that the paddler should wear a wet suit if the combined temperature of air and water add up to less than 100°.

This is the rule for all boaters on any water: If the boat turns over, stick with the boat. Here is the only exception to this rule: In cold water near shore (within 100 ft), leave the boat and get out of the water. Once the wet, cold person is out of the water, his friends should, depending on the extent of his hypothermia, get him stripped, dried off, and into dry clothes, give him warm but not hot drinks (NOT alcoholic), feed him high-energy foods, get him into a sleeping bag and get in with him (the most popular, although not always the most effective treatment) or take him to the nearest hospital in a well-heated car. If he went canoeing alone, he's a damn fool, as is anyone who goes out in any boat on any water if he can't swim.

Anyone canoeing in New York before July 1 or for a longer period than a few sunny hours should carry a complete change of clothing in a totally waterproof bag tied into the boat. A good trick is to keep your bag in your friends' boat and their bag in your boat; maybe both boats won't tip over. We once lived in a second-floor apartment overlooking the Battenkill. On a pleasant summer afternoon, we answered a knock on the door to find a couple in their twenties in wet bathing suits and nothing else, shivering uncontrollably. The woman in particular was close to severe hypothermia, although they had encountered nothing more serious than a summer thunderstorm. They were not properly prepared. Be warned.

It used to be assumed that a fast, clear river with no human habitation upstream could safely be drunk from. Today, such water can contain *Giardia lamblia,* the cause of Giardiasis, often called "Beaver Fever" because the parasite is carried by beavers and other wildlife. It is a very serious disease; the death of one Adirondack hiker recently was attributed, at least in part, to Giardiasis. Always carry water or something to drink; never, no matter how thirsty, drink out of any stream.

Beginners usually fear being swept over a dam or a waterfall. The editor once escorted a group of teenagers who had this fear to a great degree, even though they were paddling upstream at the time. Waterfalls and dams betray their presence by two signs: The water usually, although not always, becomes deeper and quieter well in advance of the hazard, and it is apparent, looking ahead, that the terrain suddenly becomes much lower. Where the hazard is a dam or an abrupt falls, there is a telltale straight line across the horizon ahead, where the river disappears. Once seen, this line can never be forgotten. In most cases (Niagara Falls is one exception), current does not speed up greatly many feet upstream of the drop, and it is possible to get over to the side and stop.

Many people suppose that rapids, waterfalls, and dams are the chief hazards in canoeing. As a matter of fact, novice canoeists usually have a healthy fear of such dangers, and most people, although not all, who canoe white water are sufficiently skilled and well prepared. Far more boaters are killed on lakes than on rivers, and little creeks can be as dangerous as big rivers. Lake Ontario or Erie, more than a half mile or so from land, is *never* the place for an open canoe. The paddler should be especially alert when the wind is offshore; that is, blowing off the land out onto the water. The water close to him may look calm, but he can be blown away from land into large waves very quickly.

Small streams offer different hazards from large rivers, but sweepers, strainers, down trees and barbed wire can be as life-threatening as rapids and haystacks. A sweeper is a tree hanging over the water with branches which make every attempt to sweep the unwary paddler out of his canoe. If the water is higher, or the tree lower, a sweeper becomes a strainer, which allows water but not canoeists to pass through. It is entirely possible for a canoeist to be pulled under water and held there by a strainer until he loses any further interest in the proceedings. Strainers and sweepers must be paddled around or carried around; a simple log down across the stream can sometimes be stood on and the canoe pulled over, but the balancing act required thereby is worthy of a circus. Farmers constantly feel that small streams are improved by barbed wire or other fencing across them.

Like a motorist, a canoeist should always be prepared to, and able to, stop suddenly. No one should ever be too proud to stop, get out, and scout the section ahead, nor should he be too proud to carry around an obstacle or line down a rapids. Lining down is almost self-explanatory: the canoeist is on shore or in the shallows with a long rope guiding the empty canoe, which finds its own way down the rapids. The ability of canoes to navigate without their masters can be quite irritating.

In passing, it might be mentioned that a canoe should always have a short length (perhaps ten feet) of line attached to the bow, and a longer length attached to the stern. These lines should not trail in the water, but should be so arranged that they will trail if the boat swamps or capsizes. Fastening lines very sketchily to the decks with masking tape will usually do the trick. The lines should *not* have knots or loops in them.

Paddlers with Physical Disabilities

Many Americans have physical disabilities, ranging from arthritis to total loss of function in the lower limbs, or worse. In earlier times, we assumed that such people could not engage in most athletic or outdoor activities. Today we are used to seeing wheelchair basketball and the like on television, but many paddlers who are not handicapped do not realize that canoeing and kayaking are sports that physically disabled persons can readily enjoy. Those who never paddled before, as well as those who were canoeists before their disability, can adapt fairly easily and quickly to paddling under changed circumstances. They may need a small amount of help from friends who paddle, some adaptive equipment, and some training.

Information on this subject can be obtained from:

American Canoe Association
Disabled Paddlers Committee
P.O. Box 1190
Newington, VA 22122-1190

How to Read this Guide

The intention of the editor was to make this canoe guide as clear, simple, straightforward, accurate, and helpful as humanly possible. Each entry, which represents a trip which can be done in one day, is organized in the same fashion, beginning with a table of the most essential information:

Name of waterway
County or counties in which this segment is located
A: segment of the waterway described
B: length of trip in miles
C: number of feet of drop from launch to takeout
D: degree of difficulty at medium high water
E: important problems the paddler is likely to encounter
F: USGS topographic quadrant(s) needed; page(s) in DeLorme Atlas
G: name of the person or persons who contributed the description.

It is worth noting that the entries apply only to the segment under discussion, NOT to the whole river. For example, C divided by B equals the average gradient for this trip, not for the entire river. Gradient, while useful, can be misleading. Much of the drop may be in dams or waterfalls to be carried around. The difficulty of rapids depends in part on gradient, in part on the volume of water, and in part on the nature of the bottom.

With regard to B, the editor knows of no precise way of measuring the length of a meandering stream, since maps often fail to show each and every bend. Distances given are the best approximation available. C is also approximate; when the contour interval is the usual 20 ft, feet of drop can theoretically be wrong by a number approaching 40 ft, although it is seldom that far off.

D uses the well-known international scale to classify white water, Class I to Class VI; it is of course subjective, as any description of rapids must be subjective, but it is the best we have. It is found on p *18.* The listing given is the highest to be encountered under normal circumstances. That is, Class III means that some of the trip is that difficult, although parts of it may be Class II or even easier.

Following the table, **Launch** gives information about the launch point, including how to get there from a nearby main highway. **Description** is a brief discussion of the trip and the area. **Takeout** tells about how and where to get the boats out of the water at the end of the trip. **Caution, Note,** and **Camping** are self-explanatory.

Launch and take-out points, as well as parking places, so far as humanly possible, have been determined to be legal and feasible. Generally speaking, wherever a public highway crosses a stream it is legal to launch or take out, since a right-of-way extends beyond the road for twenty feet or more on either side. This question is still being debated, however; we strongly recommend that you do not trespass on posted land, nor park anywhere that is not obviously a public parking place. It is astonishing how often a polite request for permission will have favorable results. If no canoeists were ever rowdy or ever littered, as most do not, permission might be granted even more often. A paddler who sees another paddler misbehave and says nothing does not help our cause. Try always to carry out a little *more* trash than you carried in.

MAPS: The US Geological Survey is engaged in publishing a series of 7.5 minute topographic quadrants covering the entire state of New York, superseding the old 15-minute quadrants. For the area dealt with in this guide, this task is virtually complete. Maps referred to in F by name are the quadrants that cover the section of waterway in question.

Very few items are as useful to a canoeist as topographic maps. They are an invaluable supplement to any guidebook, and we cannot urge too strongly that canoeists acquire the pertinent quadrants and learn how to read them, especially with regard to contour lines. Their use could prevent an unexpected encounter with a dam or waterfall.

The other map reference is to a page or pages in the *New York State Atlas and Gazetteer* published by DeLorme Mapping Company. This atlas, much used by outdoorsmen, is particularly valuable, in conjunction with a road map, in locating a specific stream. It can also be used to locate campgrounds or similar facilities in the vicinity of a waterway.

The sketch maps which accompany the text are for illustrative purposes only. They are frequently not drawn to scale, and are not intended to be used as substitutes for the appropriate USGS topographic maps.

ABBREVIATIONS: Most of the abbreviations, like mi for mile or RR for railroad, are standard and obvious. We have attempted to use N and S, L and R for directions: turn N; but north and south, left and right when used as adjectives: the north end of the lake. In the name of a town, we use a period: S. Edmeston. L always means to the left side of the paddler when facing downstream. On lakes, we have avoided L and R to the degree possible, although most lakes do have a direction of flow. I-81 is fairly obvious, Rt 13 is a state highway, as opposed to County Rt 25, although it is often difficult and sometimes impossible to determine from a map whether 34, for example, is a county or a state highway.

Not all paddlers are male, far from it, and we say, "*Vive la difference!*" However, we find it clumsy constantly to write "he or she, his or her." Thus we have chosen to refer to all "persons of indeterminate sex" as he.

Lee Clark

An uncharacteristically placid part of the East Branch of Fish Creek.

Glossary

Not many highly technical terms are used in this book; most of these are self-explanatory or explained in the text as they arise. Here are a few that may need definition:

above On moving water, this term always means upstream. "Above the bridge" is upriver from it, not up in the air.

below Opposite of above. (see above)

braided, braiding Streams divide into two, three, or more channels around obstacles. From high above this looks remarkably like braiding, the term often used to describe it.

carry To transport a boat around an obstacle, on foot or with a vehicle. Sometimes called *portage* but, curiously, seldom in the Adirondacks.

chute Essentially, a large vee. (See *vee,* on page 14.)

confluence Point at which two streams join. If one is much larger, this is not a confluence, but the mouth of the smaller. The Tioughnioga River begins at the *confluence* of the East Branch and the West Branch; the *mouth* of Ouleout Creek is the point at which it flows into the Susquehanna River.

creek It should perhaps be noted that "creek," "river," and the like are arbitrary and relative terms. Mad River is a tributary of Fish Creek. Creek is pronounced "crick" by the vast majority of central and western New York paddlers.

eddy When moving water flows *around* an obstacle, like a bridge abutment, a back current flowing upstream occurs behind the obstacle. Some eddies offer the opportunity to pause or get out of a stream, but strong and turbulent eddies can be hazardous.

eddy line When there is an eddy, there is a clear-cut visible line between water which is flowing upstream and that which is flowing down. Deliberately paddling the bow across this line is executing an eddy turn.

eddy turn A fast way to change direction. Accidentally getting in this position can cause an upset.

haystack or standing wave When moving water flows *over* an obstacle, such as a boulder, a wave is formed just downstream of the obstacle. The water is moving through the wave form; the wave stays in the same position. Small ones are fun to pass through; large ones can fill an open boat instantly.

hole or souse hole When moving water flows over a high obstacle like a dam or waterfall, a huge eddy is created all along the bottom of the obstacle. Many paddlers call this a hole or souse hole; some refer to it as a reversal, hydraulics or hydraulic. Large ones, once gotten into, are impossible to get out of. Inexperienced boaters have many times rowed, paddled, or even motored upstream too close to a dam and been caught and sucked under the falls.

riffle A very small rapids. One paddler's riffle is another's rapids.

rock garden A collection of boulders, usually not huge, forming a rapids. Usually this term refers to a situation in which the water level is low enough that the canoeist must pick his way through the rocks rather than going right over them.

shuttle A term which refers to the necessity of planning in advance to have at least one vehicle waiting at the takeout point. It is surprising how difficult this idea can be to explain to newcomers; it is even more surprising how often experienced paddlers arrive at the vehicle only to find that its keys are locked inside it or back at the launch point.

spotting The procedure of placing a vehicle, in advance, where the paddlers plan to take out, or at some intermediate point.

surfing Usually done by kayakers, this is playing on standing waves just as surfboarders play on moving waves.

swamping Usually done by canoeists, this is filling the boat with water, often by going through a standing wave without hitting any solid obstacle.

vee Water flowing between two obstacles, such as boulders, will make an obvious V-shaped pattern. Steering toward vees will generally get the canoeist through rapids.

Organization of the Book

Rivers are grouped herein by watersheds, beginning with the most important, starting at its source, then dealing with its tributaries, then their tributaries. Tributaries are discussed in the order in which they enter the main river, starting with the one farthest upstream. That is, the entries dealing with the Susquehanna, beginning with Otsego Lake, are followed by the entry dealing with Ouleout Creek, then the Unadilla River, then the Chenango River, then the tributaries of the Chenango.

The area covered by this volume is western and central New York. The western, northern, and southern boundaries of this area are easily defined: Lake Erie and the Niagara River, Lake Ontario, and Pennsylvania. Its southeastern boundary has been arbitrarily declared to be the division between the Delaware and Susquehanna watersheds. North of the Delaware we include some but not all of the canoeable streams flowing into the Mohawk or westward off the Tug Hill plateau into Lake Ontario. Streams in these categories not included in this volume will be found in *Adirondack Canoe Waters: South and West Flow* by Alec C. Proskine, published by the Adirondack Mountain Club. A couple of streams, Fish Creek and the Salmon River, are in both books because they are great favorites with Central New York as well as Adirondack canoeists.

The drainage pattern of the area covered is unusual, being generally south, west, north, and east away from the center. This would not be unusual at all if a large range of mountains were found in the center of the area. Instead, the center is occupied by a group of lakes and a man-made feature, the New York State Barge Canal, into which the Finger Lakes eventually drain. The groupings in this book, in the order included, are the Susquehanna Watershed, which occupies the southeastern corner of the area and flows generally south; the Allegheny Watershed in the southwestern part of New York, which flows generally southwest; a few streams which flow into Lake Erie; a tremendous number which flow into Lake Ontario, described from west to east; and the Barge Canal/Finger Lakes drainage area, described from east to west.

Man-made classifications are arbitrary. Does the Genesee belong in the Barge Canal group, since it intersects and feeds the canal, or the Lake Ontario Watershed, since it flows into the lake at Rochester? We have arbitrarily chosen the latter. We could have organized rivers in many ways—from the largest to the smallest, from the easiest to the hardest, or a common choice, alphabetically. We chose this system because we believe most canoeists would prefer to find West Valley Creek in the immediate vicinity of the Allegheny River in the book as it is in fact.

Acknowledgments

The real work of this guide was done by a host of volunteers, who cheerfully ran rivers, wrote reports, reran, rewrote, did car scouting, and accepted criticism and suggestions without any complaint. (Well, hardly any.) Their names, except for a few who wished to remain anonymous, appear with their contributions. Special thanks are due to "straw bosses" Daan Zwick and Alice Broberg, and to the Ka-Na-Wa-Ke Canoe Club of Syracuse. Numerous Department of Environmental Conservation rangers, park and town officials, and total strangers whose names I don't know answered innumerable questions, even though the questions often seemed stupid and the answers obvious to them. Special thanks are due to the NYS Department of Environmental Conservation's Division of Water for the watershed maps at the beginning of each segment.

Janet Zeller, chairman of the National Disabled Paddlers Committee of the American Canoe Association, herself disabled, furnished valuable information on that subject, and Frank Trerise gave me firsthand experience with the same topic. Don Otey, who is the author of several whitewater guides and, by a happy coincidence, lives next door to me, gave invaluable assistance.

Finally, Carmen Elliott, past publications director of the Adirondack Mountain Club, was a rock of stability in the ever-changing and treacherous Class V currents of creating such a guide as this. Without her professionalism, enthusiasm, and constant support this guide probably would not have been written, and certainly would have contained a great many more commas and however's.

International Scale of River Difficulty

Class I Moving water with a few riffles and small waves. Few or no obstructions.

Class II Easy rapids with waves up to three feet and wide, clear channels that are obvious without scouting. Some maneuvering is required.

Class III Rapids with high, irregular waves often capable of swamping an open canoe. Narrow passages that often require complex maneuvering. May require scouting from shore.

Class IV Long, difficult rapids with constricted passages that often require precise maneuvering in very turbulent waters. Scouting from shore is often necessary, and conditions make rescue difficult. Generally not possible for open canoes. Boaters in covered canoes and kayaks should be able to Eskimo roll.

Class V Extremely difficult, long, and very violent rapids with highly congested routes which nearly always must be scouted from shore. Rescue conditions are difficult and there is a significant hazard to life in event of a mishap. Ability to Eskimo roll is essential for kayaks and canoes.

Class VI Difficulties of Class V carried to the extreme of navigability. Nearly impossible and very dangerous. For teams of experts only, after close study and with all precautions taken.

Two Late Notes

A severe ice storm in the Rochester area during the winter of 1991 caused thousands of trees and limbs to fall. For the next several years, especially in Monroe and Livingston counties, paddlers should expect to encounter more than the usual number of down trees in waterways.

It appears that, since the tragic collapse of a Thruway bridge in 1987, New York State, counties, and local municipalities have been engaged in more than the usual number of bridge repairs. In many cases, bridges carrying minor roads have been closed and apparently will not soon be reopened. Canoeists should be prepared to find that the shortest highway route isn't, because the bridge is out.

All persons involved in the preparation of this guide have made every effort to provide accurate information, but circumstances change. We hope that readers will send any and all suggestions for the improvement of the next edition to:

Canoe Guides
Adirondack Mountain Club
RR 3, Box 3055
Lake George, NY 12845-9523

Susquehanna Watershed
Part I

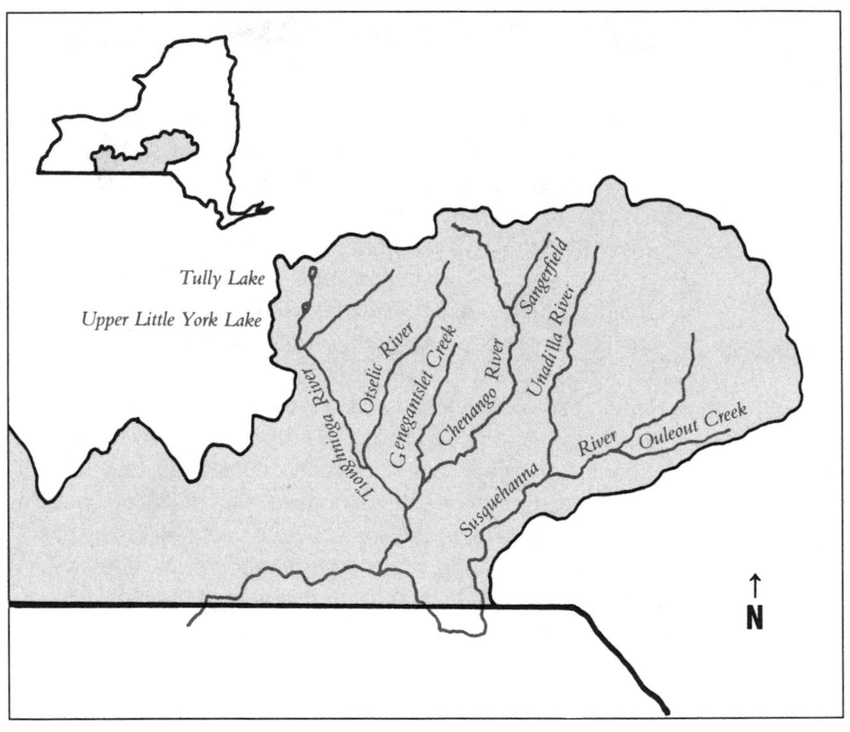

Susquehanna River

County: Otsego

Segment Cooperstown (Otsego Lake Outlet) to Milford

Length 15 mi

Drop 40 ft

Difficulty Class I

Problems Carry at Mill St. dam, sweepers, strainers

Maps Cooperstown, Milford; DeLorme p 64

Contributor Kevin Howells

Launch The Otsego Lake access site is reached by taking Rt 80 S and E to Cooperstown, where it becomes Lake St. When 80 turns S again, the canoeist stays on Lake St 2 blocks, turns L on Pioneer St and continues to the lake. Parking is available at the launch site. Rt 28 parallels the river in its early stages, providing easy access at many places.

Description The Susquehanna is the longest river rising in New York, but more of its length is in Pennsylvania and Maryland than in the Empire State. Its sources are the various creeks flowing into Otsego Lake, and it empties into Chesapeake Bay. In addition to its considerable historic importance, it is a pleasant, not too difficult paddle for most of its length. The few obstacles and difficulties encountered are, for the most part, man-made.

Historically, Otsego Lake is the "Glimmerglass" of James Fenimore Cooper's novels and the site of an unusual 18th-century military maneuver. In 1779, in order to get his heavily loaded bateaux downstream, General James Clinton dammed the outlet of the lake. When he deemed the water level high enough, he ordered the nervous paddlers into their boats, then had the dam torn out. Surprisingly, it worked.

The Susquehanna has a remarkable number of canoeable tributaries attractive to canoeists. Reading from E to W, the Unadilla and Chenango rivers flow directly into the Susquehanna, the Otselic flows into the Tioughnioga, and the Tioughnioga is a tributary of the Chenango. All four flow roughly S, all are fairly clear and fast, but without any really heavy rapids, and each has its supporters. All are described in the following pages. Smaller tributaries such as Cherry Valley, Oaks, Schenevus (Sken-ee-vus), Charlotte, and Ouleout (Ollie-out) creeks also invite paddlers but require thorough scouting and plenty of carries. Generally speaking, they are narrow, fast, and tricky in their upper reaches, with plenty of log jams. Access is often a problem; a trip may involve getting into the creek 5 mi or so above the river and canoeing down into the river and on downstream to a river access point.

To canoeists the most important event involving the Susquehanna is the annual 70-mi Memorial Day race from Cooperstown to Bainbridge. While this is considered a flatwater race, it is not for the faint of heart. There are professional classes, and the current record for 70 mi of relatively flat water is well under seven hours. There are sweepers, strainers, shallows and riffles to consider and dams to carry around, but the most stimulating part of the race is a sort of LeMans start, unique to this race so far as the editor knows. At the starting gun, as many as one hundred canoes spread out across the lake sprint for the narrow outlet a quarter mile from the line. Speed, maneuvering skill, and karate determine who the lead teams will be.

Susquehanna River • Otsego Lake Launch Site

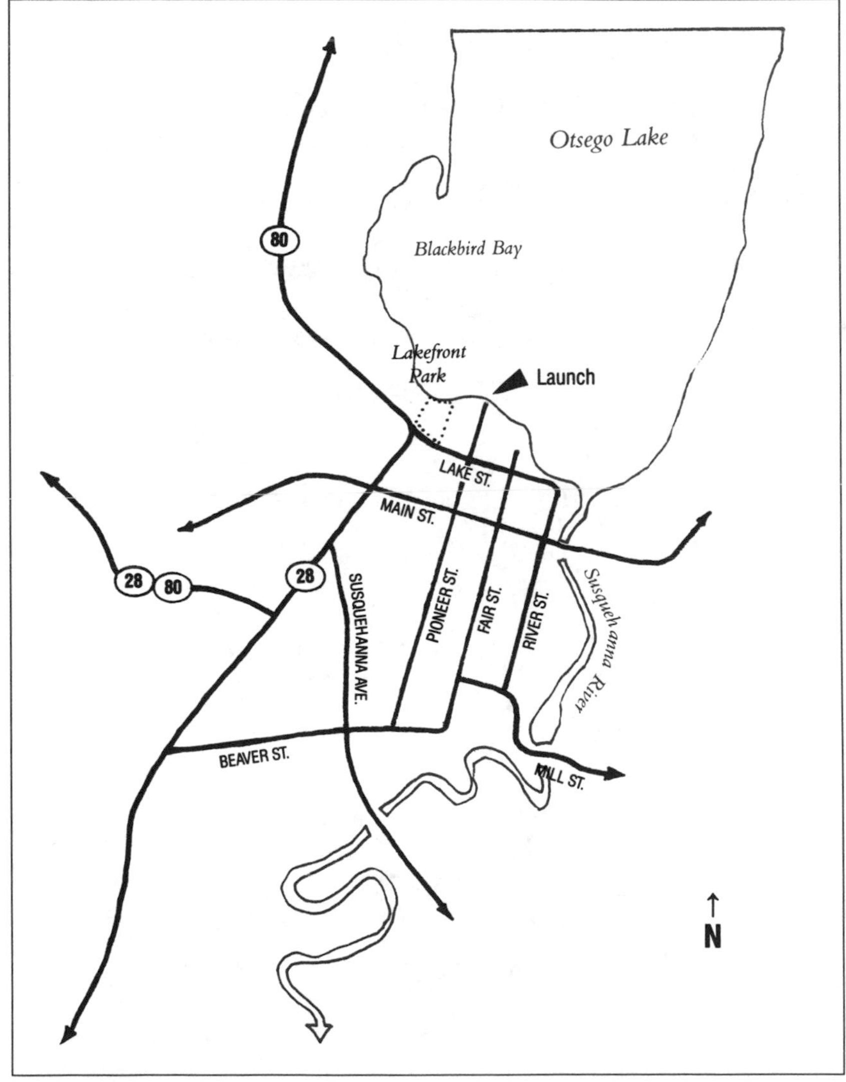

Susquehanna River • Cooperstown–Milford

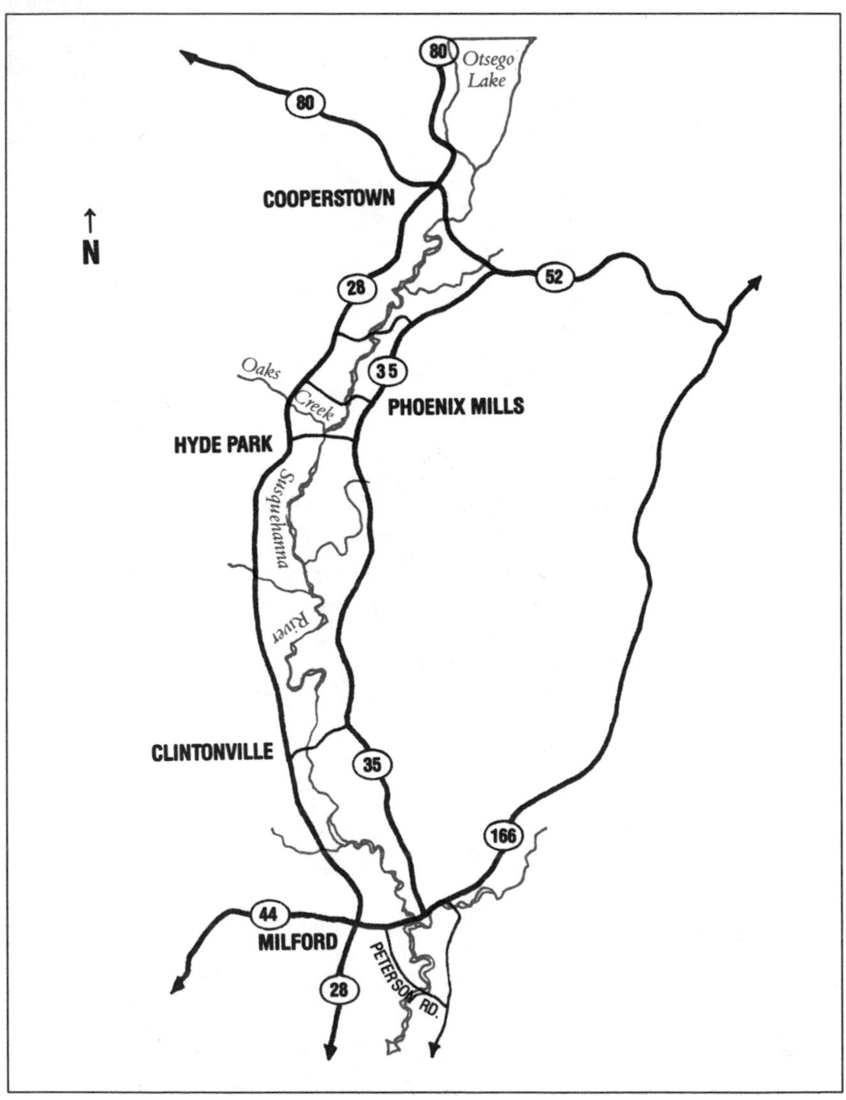

From launch, the route keeps the lakeshore R a short distance to the outlet. The entrance passes between trees and lovely homes and under Main St, the first of many bridges. Before the first mile has been completed, it is necessary to carry over Mill St dam. Passing under Susquehanna Ave, the river becomes a winding creek, with several bridges and overhanging branches which occasionally become strainers. At about the 6-mi point, the Hyde Park Bridge is reached, and Oaks Creek enters R. Nearly the same size as the river itself at this point, the creek adds substantially more water. From here to Milford, the meanders are a little less tight.

Takeout Rt 166 crosses the river near Milford and is reached from Rt 28. Takeout is on L side of river, upstream. There is adequate parking.

Camping ▲ Ringwood Farms Campground (commercial) is at the north end of Otsego Lake; Glimmerglass State Park is on Hyde Bay on the same lake.

Susquehanna River

County: Otsego

Segment ↕ Milford to Goodyear Dam

Length ↔ 12 mi

Drop ↘ Negligible

Difficulty ① Class I

Problems ✻ Possible wind on lake

Maps Milford; DeLorme p 64

Contributor Kevin Howells

Launch Access is at the Rt 166 bridge. (See preceding entry.)

Description This 12-mi trip is good for midsummer when rivers become scratchy, since the dam which creates Goodyear Lake backs up water almost to the launch point. The river meanders through a wide valley, with Crumhorn Mountain rising steeply to almost 2000 ft on the east and Red Ridge Hill, a little lower and less steep, to the west. The bridge at Portlandville, 8 mi from launch, marks the beginning of the lake proper. From here the canoeist should hug the left shore at first; the open water ahead looks tempting but is actually a dead end. Once around the peninsula and close to the true east shore, the preferred route crosses to the other shore and hugs that until the telltale horizon line of a dam is seen ahead and the east shore closes in. At this point the canoeist *must* take out L.

Routes 28 and 35 parallel the widened river, one on each side. A good access point is a state boat launch site at Crumhorn Landing on Rt 35 about 5 mi S of its junction with 166. There are no legal public access points between here and the dam, although it would be possible to take out on either side of Goodyear Lake in an emergency. If it appears that wind will be a problem on the lake, or that the carry around the dam is too rigorous, canoeists should get out at Crumhorn Landing.

Takeout The carry around the dam, part of the Memorial Day Race, is a fairly rugged one, but at least recreational canoeists won't have to run. The takeout for this is at the tip of the point dividing the channel leading to the dam from the dead end. The .25-mi carry goes steeply up from the lake, around

Susquehanna River • Milford–Goodyear Dam

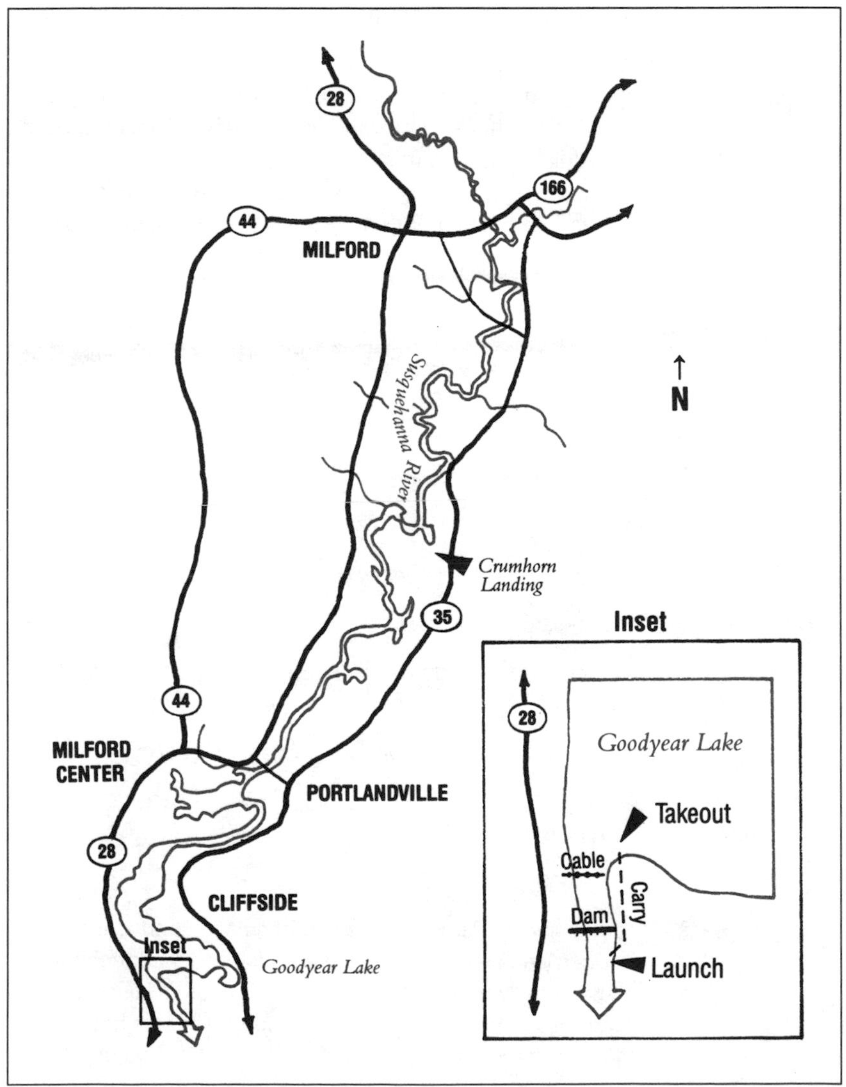

the east end of the dam, then steeply down with poor footing to rejoin the river.

Caution Do not paddle past this point to the dam; there is no egress there. A cable across the water joining white floats makes it impossible to make a mistake.

Less hardy souls may wish to take out at Crumhorn Landing and make a car carry to a launch point described in the next entry.

Susquehanna River

Counties: Otsego, Delaware

Segment Goodyear Dam to Otego

Length 20 mi

Drop 100 ft if launch is just below dam

Difficulty Class I except as noted

Problems One short mild rapids below Rt 23; mild rapids and a dam above

Maps Milford, W. Davenport, Oneonta, Otego; DeLorme pp 64, 50, 49

Contributor Kevin Howells

Launch It is possible to launch immediately below Goodyear Dam after carrying around it. (See previous entry.) Launch here can be slightly tricky because of mild rapids, or quite difficult if water is being released from the dam, which is not a common occurrence except at race time. A mile or so below

Goodyear Lake I-88 crosses the Susquehanna, and from this point it parallels the river for 45 mi to Harpursville, providing a pleasant view of the stream most of the time as well as access near most interchanges. Rt 7 runs parallel to I-88 for most of this distance; frequently one highway is on each side of the river. There are many state public access sites, some but not all of which are described below.

Description About .5 mi below the dam comes the infamous shortcut R which saves 30 seconds and has wrecked many a canoe. One mile farther Rt 7 crosses. Those who shun the carry around the dam may choose to launch at the public access site here. Three miles farther at Emmons is another such site at Stillwater Rd off I-88 Exit 16. From above Oneonta to well below it, the river can be scouted easily from I-88, provided that a passenger, not the driver, does the scouting. Steady current and riffles continue 1 mi to the F & F Airpark, where Charlotte Creek enters L. For the next mile the current is strong; at H water waves can be big enough to put some water into an open canoe. Oneonta Dam, a low dam 2 mi farther, can be carried R.

About 2 mi beyond the dam the river steepens briefly, forming a minor rapid, considered to be Class I on the left but Class II for those who choose to run it on the right. Just below the rapid is a state boat launch site R, about at the Rt 205 bridge and I-88 interchange. There are no rapids between this access point and the takeout. From here to Otego is not so exciting as the preceding 10 mi, but it is a very pleasant spring, summer, or fall trip on a full, moving river, paddling along beside the superhighway, passing under five bridges.

Takeout About 1 mi downstream from the village of Otego is a public launch site on river L. It is on the Otego Wells Bridge Rd about 1 mi S of the I-88 Otego exit.

Susquehanna River • Goodyear Dam–Otego

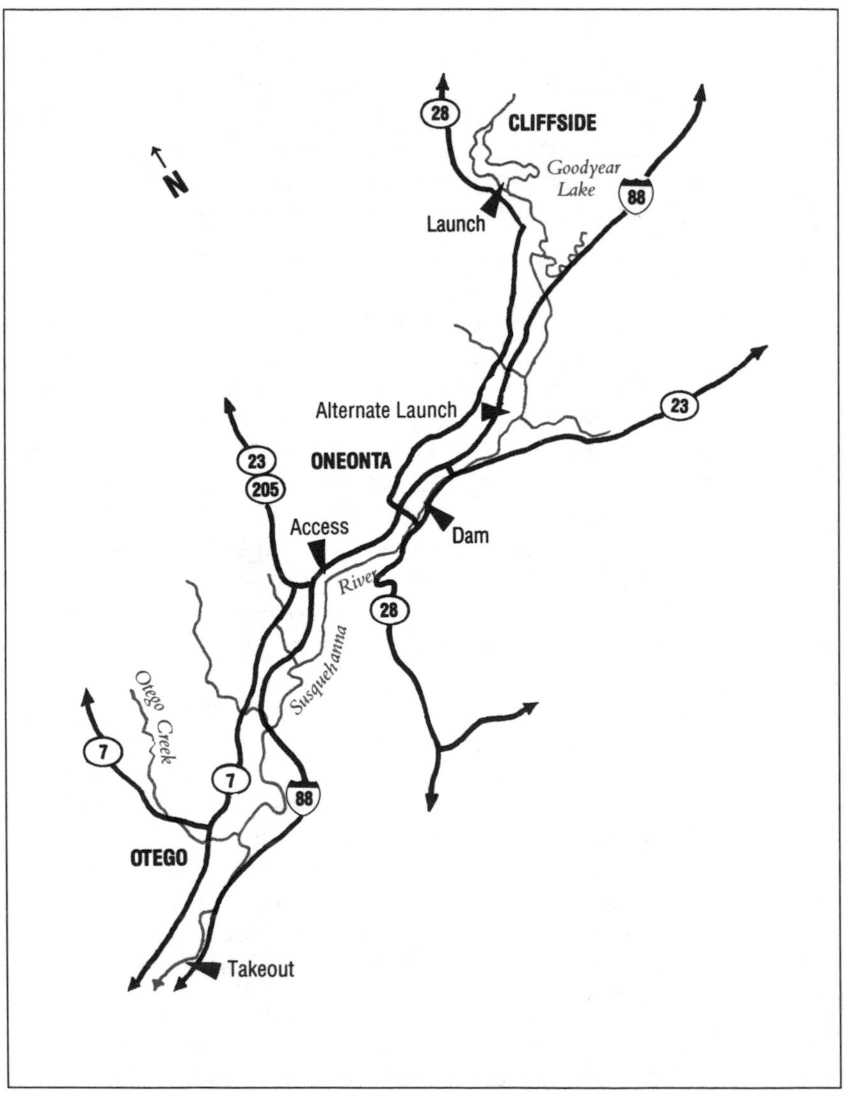

Note ☞ The River St bridge in Otego is out and apparently will not be replaced. To reach the Otego Wells Bridge Rd from Rt 7, continue SW past River St about 1 mi, turn L as if to reach I-88. Continue through the interchange (this is possible although it looks impossible) and turn R toward Gary Enck's Car Store. About .8 mi from here is the very attractive access point.

Camping ▲ Delaware County KOA, Franklin, is a commercial campground not far from the takeout point.

Susquehanna River

Counties: Otsego, Delaware, Chenango

Segment ↕ Otego to Bainbridge

Length ↔ 21 mi

Drop ↘ 65 ft

Difficulty ① Class I

Problems ✻ Shallows, gravel bars at M or less, broken dam at Unadilla

Maps Otego, Franklin, Unadilla, Sidney; DeLorme pp 49, 48

Contributor ✍ Kevin Howells

Launch Access is just downstream from Otego. (See preceding entry.)

Description ✏ From here down, the Susquehanna is becoming a big river; below Bainbridge it is certainly canoeable, but wide and often shallow. After it loops into Pennsylvania and returns to New York, the river is vast and the scenery mostly urban. In

Binghamton, several low dams cross the wide river. Even the section described here is broad and shallow; at less than MH water, there may be some gravel bars to avoid. During this entire trip, I-88 and Rt 7 parallel the river, one on each side, and bridges and highways dominate the scenery. Many small islands and split channels provide interest, and for the most part the shoreline greenbelt conceals the back yards and riverbank discards.

Three miles from launch the route passes under the bridge which gives the village of Wells Bridge its name; the village is mostly R. Access is also possible here, on the R, upstream. There is adequate parking, but cars must not block the clearly marked fire department water supply area. At about the 7-mi point, Rt 357 crosses the river. Just before this Ouleout Creek enters L. (See p 35.) Less than .5 mile from here, at Unadilla, the river passes over the former site of a dam, forming a Class I rapids which is easily runnable by all but beginners. It is possible to take out on the right bank a few hundred yards above the dam at Corwin Park in Unadilla. This park is on Rt 7 and parking is adequate along the highway. Unfortunately, getting out of the river up a steep but mostly grassy bank is a bit difficult, but those who wish to avoid the broken dam will find it quite possible. Beginning with Unadilla, the Susquehanna flows past three fair-sized towns in quick succession, Unadilla and Bainbridge on the right, Sidney on the left.

Below the Rt 357 bridge are two more bridges at Unadilla; the second is the relatively new spur from I-88, across the river. Just downstream of this bridge is a state boat launch site L. The river meanders more after this point, and extensive braiding just before Sidney allows racers to find a short cut. Paddlers in no hurry will probably stick to the main channel, which is readily apparent. Two bridges

Susquehanna River • Otego–Bainbridge

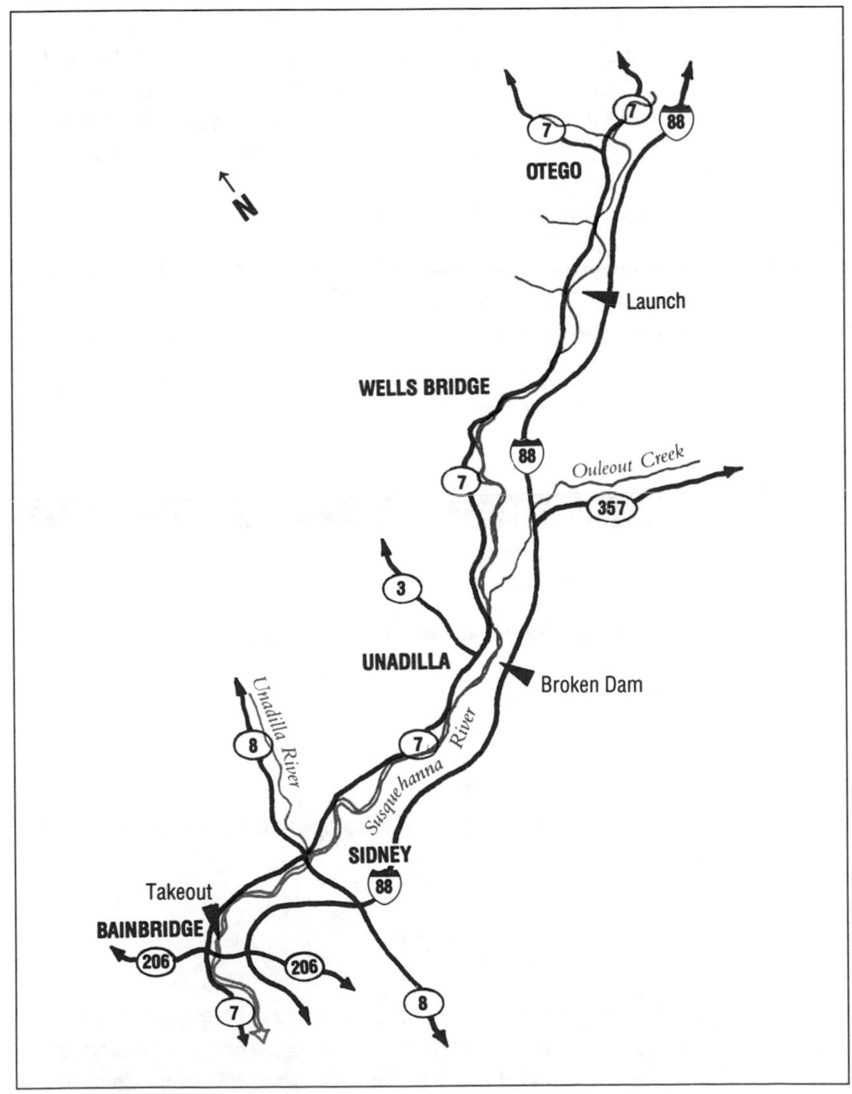

cross the river at Sidney; the Unadilla empties into the Susquehanna at the second, the Rt 8 bridge. Just below the confluence R is a state boat launch site. There are shoals to avoid in this area. About 1.5 mi farther comes a RR bridge, and 3 mi from this the trip ends at General Clinton Park, Bainbridge, which is the site of the finish line of the annual race, 70 mi from Otsego Lake.

Takeout The park is on the right, just before the Rt 206 bridge. It is reached by highway from the Bainbridge exit of I-88 by driving NW across the river to Rt 7 in the center of town, then taking Rt 7 NE a short distance to the park entrance R.

Camping ▲ See previous entry.

Ouleout Creek

County: Delaware

Segment ↕ Union Church Rd to Susquehanna River

Length ↔ 5 mi

Drop ↘ 70 ft

Difficulty ① Class I

Problems ✱ Sharp turns, fast current, possible sweepers and strainers

Maps Franklin, Unadilla; DeLorme p 49

Contributor Mark Freeman

Launch The only possible launch point is at the Union Church Rd (called locally KOA Rd) bridge. This is reached by driving E 1.8 mi from I-88 Exit 11. The left turn at this point doubles back downhill and is almost impossible not to overshoot. The bridge is at the foot of the hill; launch is on the south side downstream. There is parking room for about two cars.

Description Ouleout (Ollie-out) Creek offers delightful canoeing; unfortunately access is next to impossible. Just above the recommended launch point, a huge US Army Corps of Engineers flood control dam backs up the waters of the creek to create E. Sidney Lake. There is a public park here with all the usual facilities including a launch site (for the lake) and camping. According to a Town of Sidney official, there is no legal access to the creek above the lake. Canoeing is of course possible on the lake, which is 1.5 mi long and about .2 mi wide at its widest.

The trip described offers a short, fast, exhilarating run at H levels; it is not canoeable at much less than MH. The gradient of about 15 ft/mi is considerable but quite regular, with no sudden drops. The bottom is mostly gravel with a few small boulders. The chief difficulty lies in occasional sweepers and strainers, especially around sharp turns, but Ouleout Creek is straighter than many otherwise similar tributaries of the Susquehanna. In May 1991, no trees blocked the entire width of the stream. The banks are posted almost everywhere.

Until the first bridge the route is through woodland and fields; the paddler feels quite isolated. There are red-winged blackbirds and other birds and wildlife, but there isn't much time for gawking at the scenery. At the 3-mi point the I-88 bridge is reached; 1 mi farther is the bridge at Covered Bridge Rd, which is not a covered bridge. Here there are cottages and posted signs everywhere. From this point, the stream is straighter and more open. The paddler soon enters the Susquehanna and immediately passes under Rt 357.

Takeout The best takeout is at Corwin Park in Unadilla which is R just after the 357 bridge and just before a mild short rapids caused by a broken dam. An alternative is to run the rapids and continue to the state access point L below the I-88 spur bridge. (See p. 32.)

Unadilla River

Counties: Madison, Chenango, Otsego

Segment West Edmeston to New Berlin

Length 13 mi

Drop 48 ft

Difficulty Class I

Problems The river is full of old tires, caused by flooding of a tire dump upstream

Maps Brookfield, New Berlin N, New Berlin S; DeLorme p 63

Contributor Ron Schlie

Launch Access is at the bridge in W. Edmeston, on the Coontown Mountain Rd, which can be reached by traveling S from US 20 on Rt 8 about 8 mi, then turning E into the hamlet of W. Edmeston. Parking is not easy; for this launch point, the canoeist must park on the shoulder of the road.

Description The Unadilla, the Tioughnioga, and the Chenango, three tributaries of the Susquehanna, are all deservedly popular canoe routes. The Unadilla is usually crystal clear above New Berlin and perhaps a tad less swift-moving than the other two. On all three, birds and animals ranging from beaver to deer, from hummingbirds to hawks, may be seen, and all these streams flow, for the most part, through alternating woodland and pastureland, with a few small city or suburban vistas thrown in.

A few years ago, a paddler described this stretch of the Unadilla as almost totally lacking in man-made debris; since then, a flood has strewn the contents of a tire dump upstream all along this stretch. One contributor suggests that this is now an ideal stream for practicing paddling techniques, since the canoe will consistently bounce off rubber tires rather than rocks. Perhaps it is not too optimistic to hope that some combination of volunteer and official action will clear out the man-made hazards and let canoeists go back to hitting rocks, as nature intended.

This stretch from W. Edmeston to New Berlin is best run in fairly high water; before the advent of the tires, it was quite a pleasant trip. From the launch point to S. Edmeston, the river runs alternately through pastureland and wooded areas. At the time of writing, there were no problems in this stretch, but if the water level is low, the bottom of the canoe will acquire some scratches. Alternative access is possible at the bridge in S. Edmeston. The road which crosses this bridge appears to be County Rt 20 to the E and 25 to the W; the river divides Otsego and Chenango counties. It is often desirable to spot an intermediate vehicle at this point; if there is a moderate to strong southerly wind, this stretch can seem interminable.

From S. Edmeston to New Berlin there are numerous bends, and down trees may block all or part of the river, necessitating quick maneuvering and/or short carries. There are almost no human dwellings to be seen in this stretch; when a few houses appear, the trip is almost over.

Takeout Access is possible at the Rt 80 bridge in New Berlin, which is reached by continuing S on County Rt 8 from the launch point about 9 mi, to the intersection of 8 and 80. Continue S on 80 about .5 mi to the bridge. Access is R above the bridge and above a small tributary which enters just at the bridge. Both parking and access are better than they appear at first glance.

Unadilla River

Counties: Chenango, Otsego

Segment New Berlin to Holmesville

Length 13 mi

Drop 45 ft

Difficulty Class I

Problems Sweepers, strainers, log jams

Maps New Berlin N, New Berlin S, Holmesville; DeLorme p 63

Contributor Mark Freeman

Launch Rt 8 parallels the river W, and there are numerous access points from this highway, but see the CAUTION below. Recommended launch is at the Rt 80 bridge in New Berlin. (See preceding entry.)

Description This may seem to be the longest 13 mi ever paddled, especially if there is a strong southwest wind. For most of the trip, the river is quite wide and deep, especially at H level. Unfortunately, it frequently divides around islands, offering three or more choices. It is important to choose wisely, attempting to follow where the greatest volume of water is going. It sometimes seems that the channel that is most choked with trees to start with is the best choice in the long run.

Soon after launch, the trash-laden banks of the town are left behind, and the second bridge, at the 1-mi point, comes as a surprising reminder that the paddler is still near a town. The river is frequently braided; there is a confusing maze at about the 3.5-mi mark. One mile farther is a larger island group. At this writing, what appears to be the main channel L is totally blocked with a tree, limbs, and debris. There is a small golf course here R, and a little-used road leads from Rt 8 to an abandoned bridge to an island.

Caution ✖ This is not a good place to spot a vehicle, since the paddlers who choose the wrong channel will never go past this point.

The river continues through a wide valley, meandering from side to side. There are occasional glimpses over the high clay banks of steep wooded hills, or barns and silos. Abundant wildlife includes several species of ducks, hawks, red-winged blackbirds and other birds, woodchucks, muskrats, even a snake. At roughly 10 mi from launch, the river straightens out somewhat and Cty Rt 18 is close L. Tumbledown shacks are close to large attractive homes along the road. Just before this a state access point is R.

About 1.75 mi before takeout, the river passes under Rt 23 at S. New Berlin. Another state access point is here R, just downstream. From here the Unadilla flows quick and straight along a steep hill L, then makes a sharp right turn as the end of the trip is reached.

Takeout Ditch Rd runs E .3 mi from Rt 8 at the hamlet of Holmesville, then makes a right turn to cross the river. There is good access and good parking here on the right side of the river upstream from the bridge.

Note ☞ The Unadilla River is canoeable from here to the Susquehanna about 18 mi downstream. The current is slow and the river is wide and deep at MH or better levels; there are numerous access points and somewhat fewer meanders and snags. It is a peaceful and pleasant but not very sporty run.

Camping ▲ Hunts Pond State Park, about 3 mi SW of New Berlin, offers camping and other recreational facilities.

Chenango River

County: Chenango

Segment ↕ Sherburne to Norwich

Length ↔ 11 mi

Drop ↘ 49 ft

Difficulty ① Class I (Class II at H water level)

Problems ✲ Sweepers, strainers, often around sharp bends

Maps Hamilton, Earlville, Norwich; Delorme p 62

Contributors ✍ Ron Schlie, Charlie Murn

Launch To reach access point, drive W from village of Sherburne on Rt 80 about .75 mi. Cross the river and park on the north side of the road, where a pull-off has room for four or five cars. Launch upstream of this bridge on river R.

Description ✏ The Chenango rises in the hills around Morrisville and flows into the Susquehanna at Binghamton, 56 river miles from Sherburne. For most of its length it is a great river to canoe, moving, but not too fast (average gradient less than 5 ft/mi), with clear water and abundant wildlife. Deer, otter, beaver, hawks, owls, and many other birds are usually present; one canoeist suggests that "about the only animal you won't see is a black bear."

Sherburne to North Norwich: This section is best run at M to H water, but *not at flood level.* At launch point, L to M water level may involve some bottom scratching (of the canoe). Watch for and run vees in riffles. The abandoned Chenango Canal runs along the west side of the Chenango in this section. The river splits twice; the west (R) channel is often better. Beginners should only run this section in the company of more experienced paddlers. The Rt 12 bridge at N. Norwich, where there is a state boat launch site and a parking lot often used by fishermen, is a good spot for lunch. If it looks like a windy day, this is also a good place to park an intermediate vehicle.

North Norwich to Norwich: For about the next 3 mi, the river turns and twists, and there are several islands. Good river judgment can help select the best channel; it changes from time to time. Soon, Whapanaka Brook enters L; shortly thereafter the river flows under Whaupaunaucau Rd, proving that there's more than one way to spell an Indian name. From here on, the Chenango takes a more straightforward course. In this section, the river flows through a wide valley, and if there is a moderate to strong southerly wind, the second part of the trip can seem to last forever.

Takeout There are several access points in the vicinity of Norwich. Recommended takeout point is at the Rt 23 bridge, which is reached by driving E out of Norwich. There is a small parking lot R just before the bridge. Takeout is on river R just downstream of the bridge.

Note ☞ The Chenango is canoeable for the next 45 mi, to where it joins the Susquehanna in Binghamton. It is wide and fairly slow, with an average gradient of under 5 ft per mi. There is generally sufficient water below Norwich, except for a section near Port Crane, where it may be scratchy at ML or lower levels. There is a low dam in the Binghamton metropolitan area, just before the mouth, and the scenery in this area is urban, but from Norwich to Port Crane the vistas are primarily woods, open fields, and residential areas. There are frequent access points.

Sangerfield River (Ninemile Swamp)

Counties: Madison, Oneida

Segment ↕ Loomis Rd to Hubbardsville

Length ↔ Possible 6-7 mi round trip, depending on strength and determination

Drop ↘ About 20 ft

Difficulty ① Class I

Problems ✱ Down trees

Maps Hubbardsville; DeLorme pp 62, 63

Contributors ✍ H. Rodman, Alice Broberg

Launch It is possible to launch at the Loomis Rd or the Swamp Rd bridge, but many down trees and much barbed wire across the stream in the northern stretches make it more feasible to put in at the Wickwire Rd bridge, paddle upstream (N) as far as desired, and return. Wickwire Rd is the third right turn off Rt 12, traveling S (about 8.5 mi) from Rt 20. Parking is possible off either side of the bridge. This is an easy launch site from a sloping grassy shore; motorboat owners even back up trailers to launch here, although fishing is said to be not very good. In spring, wildflowers abound near the parking areas.

Description ✏ In spite of the many difficulties, this is a very popular trip because of its interesting plants, animals, and history. In the 19th century the notorious Loomis gang kept stolen horses (and possibly human captives) in the swamp, and hid there from pursuers. A local road and hill still bear their name. *The Loomis Gang* by George W. Walter, published in 1953, is worth reading before taking this trip—if you can find a copy. Although in many ways a swamp, the area contains large trees, both deciduous and coniferous, as well as the more usual swamp plants such as alders and waterlilies. Among the fauna are beaver and sandpipers.

The launch is into a convenient shallow eddy. From here the route is upstream against a sometimes considerable current; travel downstream from the launch point is not recommended because of the many impediments. At first the river is wide enough for several canoes to travel abreast, but the rule soon becomes single file, threading a way through alders and water plants. At H water level there is no place to step on solid ground during the trip, and lunch is eaten in the canoe. On a summer trip, picnicking is possible on a grassy shore. Very hardy souls may attempt to travel all the way to Swamp Rd, coping with man-made and beaver-made obstructions, not to mention down trees. At some point the party will turn around for the quick trip with the current back to the launch point.

Takeout Exit is at the launch point.

Genegantslet Creek

County: Chenango

Segment ↕ Smithville Flats to Rt 12

Length ↔ 8.5 mi

Drop ↘ 100 ft

Difficulty ① Class I

Problems ✲ Several tight turns, many sweepers and/or strainers

Maps Smithville Flats, Greene; DeLorme p 48

Contributor John Consler

Launch Access point is under Rt 41 bridge in Smithville Flats and is excellent for a small stream. Easiest access is slightly upstream on west side. There is ample parking here. Smithville Flats is reached by taking Rt 12 SW from Utica to Greene, then Rt 41 N from Greene. It is possible to launch at a state access site about 4 river mi upstream, but the difficulties mentioned below would be greater above Smithville Flats, and the dam which is just upstream of the Rt 41 bridge would have to be negotiated.

Description Water level is said to be perfect in the middle of April, after a heavy rain. This stream cannot be run when level is L; even at MH water, the canoe will touch rocks several times. However, at time of flood extreme caution should be used because of sweepers or strainers, which often lurk around tight bends. This is not a stream for beginners, but those canoeists who run it return again and again.

The Genegantslet (Jen-a-gan-slet) is a fast-moving,

twisting, tricky river; the channel braids into three parts several times. Runoff is rapid in the spring. When numerous sweepers and log jams are taken into consideration, the canoeist should be prepared to get wet.

About 4.5 mi from launch, the Rt 206 bridge, another possible access point, is reached. Just before this point the valley broadens, and there are numerous sycamores. After this bridge, the valley closes in again and conifers predominate. About a mile farther, an aspen grove on the east bank offers a good picnic spot. Wild onions abound here.

Takeout Rt 12 crosses Genegantslet Creek at the hamlet of Lower Genegantslet Corner. Takeout is possible just above this bridge, on the east bank. Indian Brook enters R just before this. About 1 mi downstream from the takeout point, Genegantslet Creek enters the Chenango River in a swampy delta.

Tully Lake

Counties: Cortland, Onondaga

Segment ↕ Entire lake

Length ↔ 4 mi round trip

Drop ↘ Negligible

Difficulty ① Class I

Problems Unless very windy, none

Maps Otisco Valley, Tully; DeLorme p 61

Contributors Members of the Ka-Na-Wa-Ke Canoe Club

Launch Access is easy at the state launch site at the south end of the lake. To reach this point, take I-81 S to the exit at Tully Center. Take the exit W, turn S on Rt 11A, cross Rt 80 to Lake Rd, take Lake Rd, turn L on Wetmore Rd (which becomes Saulsbury Rd), then R on Friendly Shores Rd to launch site. This takes less time to do than to read about. (See accompanying map.)

Description At this writing, Tully is an attractive small lake with good canoeing and plenty of wildlife. Much of the shoreline is developed, and more development is in progress. Almost all of the land is posted; without permission of the owner, landing is not possible. There is no public picnicking or swimming site, but there is no legal impediment to launching at the above site, paddling the lake, and eating a lunch in the canoe or at the launch site. The west shore S of Mirror Lake is wooded, and the southern marshlands area of Tully Lake, between Camp Hoover and Saulsbury Rd, is mostly unpopulated.

The route follows the east shore N to a small pond, which may be explored. Thence the west shore may be followed to a small channel under a low concrete bridge to Mirror Lake. Mirror Lake, very small and shallow, is about 40 percent developed at this writing but may become much more developed in the near future. From Mirror Lake a second small channel proceeds S to an arm of Tully Lake. This arm is largely wooded and natural. There is an island slightly E of this point, turtles may be seen, and the water is suitable for swimming. This is a good spot for a lunch stop; however, the island is privately owned and posted. There are muskrat lodges in a weedy area of the lake SE of the island.

Continuing S along the west shore, the canoeist reaches the bay at the south end of the lake. A channel here leads to

Tully Lake • Entire Lake

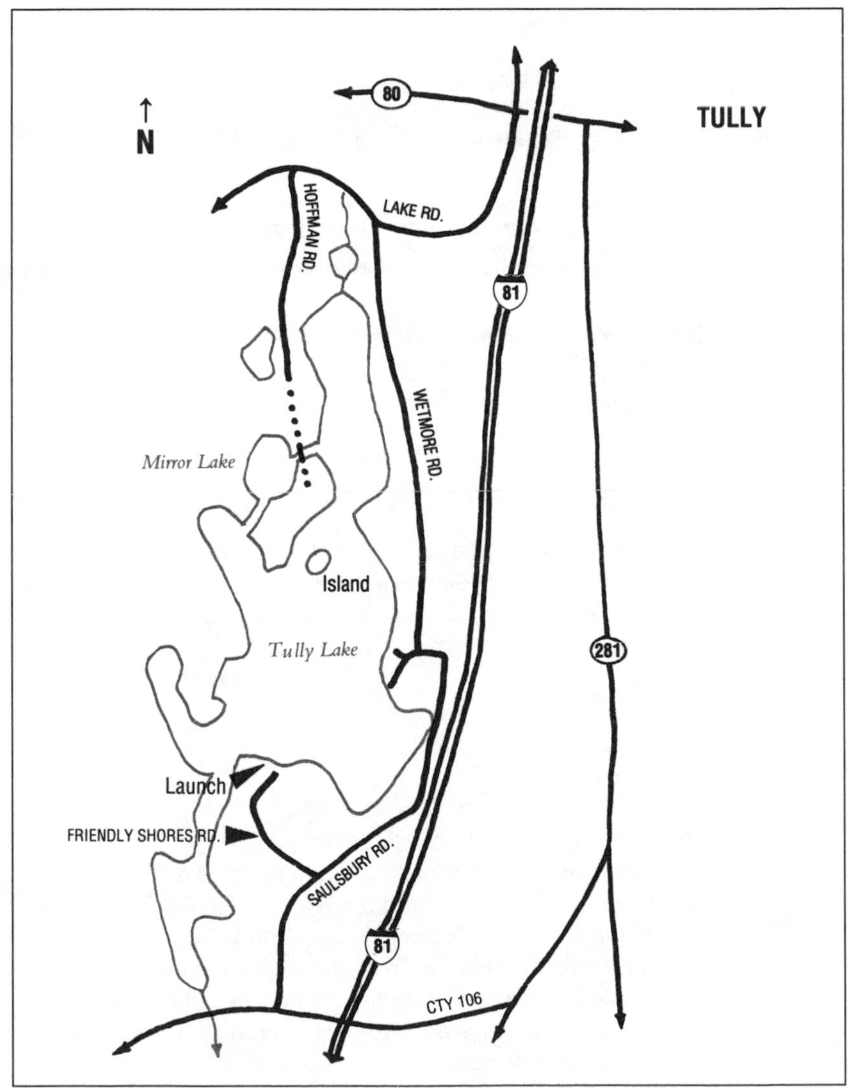

two small shallow ponds where great blue herons nest. From here the route returns to the main lake and along the east shore to the takeout point.

Takeout As with any round trip, takeout is at the launch point.

Upper Little York Lake (including Green and Goodale Lakes)

County: Cortland

Segment All three lakes in their entirety

Length 3-4 mi

Drop Negligible (see note about water level, below)

Difficulty Class I (see note about Goodale, below)

Problems Water level on Little York is intentionally lowered in October, making access to Goodale difficult. At this time, after normal canoeing season, current from Goodale can be swift, with about a 2-ft drop in 200 yds

Maps Homer; DeLorme p 61

Contributor Byron L. Craft

Launch The easiest way to get to the only public launch on the lake is to get off I-81 at the interchange just N of Preble. Travel S on Rt 281 about 3 mi to the sign for Dwyer Memorial (Cortland County) Park on the L. There is a pavilion to the R inside the park entrance. Just beyond the pavilion and before the creek is the road to the launch site, a broad flat area providing very easy access and adequate parking.

Description Upper Little York Lake, the source of the West Branch of the Tioughnioga, was called just Little York Lake when the contributor was a boy. With a shore lined with summer cottages (except at the shallow south end) and good bass fishing, it was a great place for a ten-year-old to have his first canoe experience. Happily, it has changed little since then.

After launching, follow the shore line, first S, then bending N. Soon, the entrance to Goodale Lake is reached. This route passes under I-81 and the railroad. Goodale contains many attractive islets and the area abounds in interesting plants and birds. Returning to Little York the route continues S about a mile to the dam and back up to the park.

Green Lake is at the north edge of the park, and may be seen by crossing the creek beyond the pavilion. Access to Green is from the parking lot. Although quite small, this lake is also a very attractive place for canoeing. It is 3-5 ft higher than the other two. Its outlet is totally non-canoeable.

Takeout As with most lake trips, takeout is at the launch point, whether the trip was on Green or Little York.

West Branch, Tioughnioga River

County: Cortland

Segment Durkee Pool to junction with East Branch

Length 6.5 mi

Drop 20 ft

Difficulty Class I

Problems Several bridges in Homer, a low dam, down trees

Maps Otisco Valley, Homer, Cortland; DeLorme p 61

Contributor Byron L. Craft

Launch The town of Homer is reached by driving S on I-81 from Syracuse. Unfortunately, there is no longer any legal access to the West Branch N of Durkee Memorial Pool, which is on the north side of Homer, although the canoeist may catch tantalizing glimpses of the stream through the fence that borders the Interstate. Durkee Pool is an old gravel quarry; access is feasible here, over 8- to12-inch-high banks. Access is also theoretically possible, but not recommended, at several bridges between Durkee Pool and the takeout point.

Description The West Branch of the Tioughnioga River has its source in the group of lakes that includes Tully and flows S through the Little York Lake group. While these lakes are canoeable (see pp 45–49), the West Branch is not navigable much above Homer. Ambitious paddlers may go upstream .5 to 1 mi from the launch point, but the current is strong and obstructions soon occur. Going downstream, the swift current requires the canoeist to be alert to duck under each of the five bridges. Just S of Homer, a low dam may be portaged on either side. There are often down trees to negotiate as well; while this could not be classified as a whitewater run, the narrowness of the stream, swift current, and numerous impediments make it no trip for a beginner. This trip affords a splendid view of the back yards of Homer and Cortland; otherwise it is not very scenic.

Takeout Continue S to the junction and paddle up the East Branch a very short distance to the takeout at Yaman Park off Rt13 in Cortland. (See p 54.)

East Branch, Tioughnioga River

County: Cortland

Segment ↕ Cuyler to Truxton

Length ↔ 5.5 mi

Drop ↘ 30 ft

Difficulty ① Class I

Problems ✻ Likelihood of down trees

Maps Cuyler, Truxton; DeLorme p 61

Contributors ✍ Members of the Ka-Na-Wa-Ke Canoe Club

Launch Take Rt. 13 to Cuyler from north or south. Launch at the Tripoli Rd bridge between Tripoli and Cuyler, as shown on sketch map. Parking is possible away from the bridge on the shoulder of the road. If the water is high enough, launch is possible into the East Branch of Tioughnioga Creek at the next bridge upstream, known locally as the E. Keeney Rd.

Description Several streams join near Cuyler to form the East Branch of the Tioughnioga River. They include the east, west, and middle branches of Tioughnioga Creek. Although the East Branch of the river is more commonly paddled from Truxton to Cortland, this upper section, while comparable in wildlife and scenery, is of course narrower, has more riffles and is much prettier. It makes a relaxing short run. It can only be run at MH or better water level, but it is generally good in a normal spring or fall or in summer after a rainy spell. The gradient is slight and runoff is slow.

Both Rt 13 and the railroad follow the East Branch for most of its length. The stream passes under the highway

East Branch, Tioughnioga River • Cuyler to Truxton

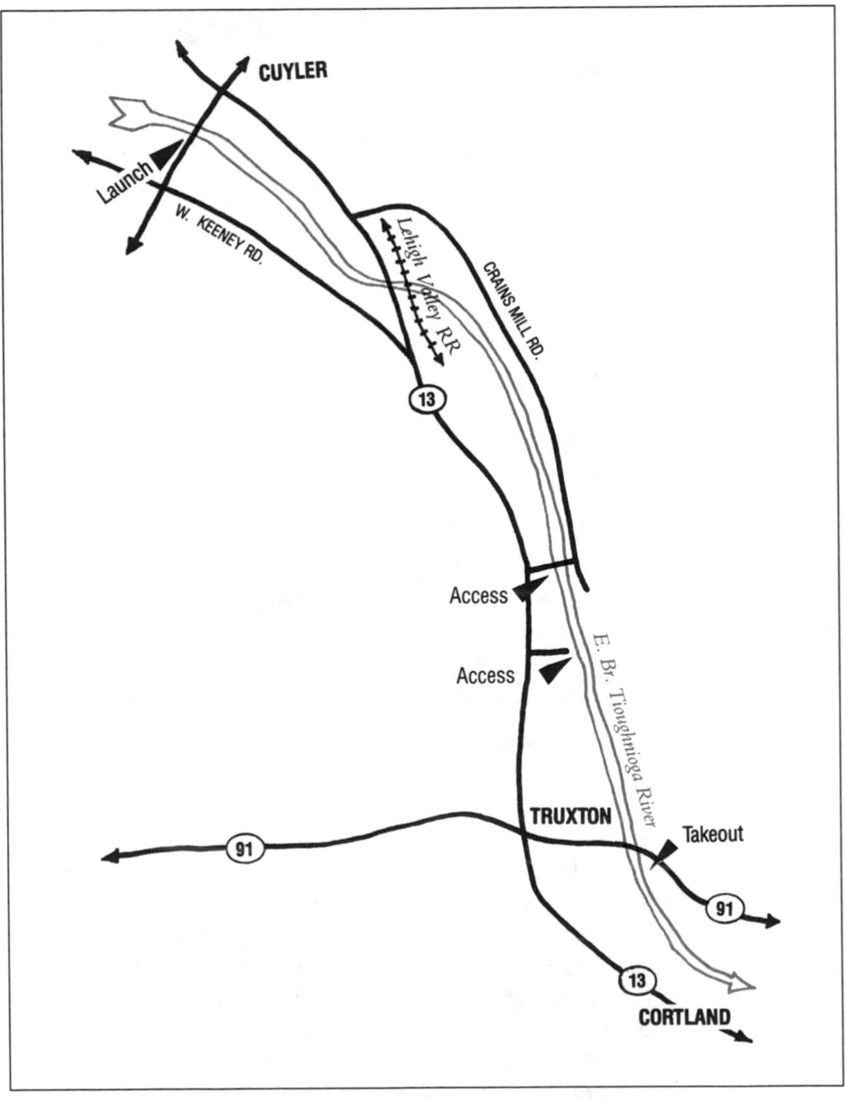

about 1.75 mi from the launch point and under the RR bridge soon thereafter. The waterway meanders through a wide valley, with fairly steep slopes on either side of the valley. At about the 3-mi point the valley narrows, then widens again.

Takeout Access is possible at either point shown on the sketch map or at McGraw Field in Truxton. (John McGraw, the great baseball manager of the early days, was a native of Truxton.) McGraw Field is just S of Rt 13 on Rt 91. Just downstream of the bridge, at the ballfield, is a small dock which offers excellent access. There is adequate parking, but access may be restricted at times to permit Fire Service tank trucks to take on water.

East Branch, Tioughnioga River

County: Cortland

Segment ↕ Truxton to Cortland

Length ↔ 14 mi

Drop ↘ 65 ft

Difficulty ① Class I

Problems ✻ One or more strainers; log across stream

Maps Truxton, Homer, Cortland; DeLorme p 61

Contributors Bill Fuller and others

Launch There are access points in several places where bridges cross the stream; one of the best is at the ball park in Truxton. (See preceding entry.)

Description This stretch of the East Branch consists of a long series of oxbows surrounded by cropland in the middle of a wide valley. The upper section is very crooked and narrow; much maneuvering is required. Soon after launch, Labrador Brook enters R and, at about the 1-mi point, Kenney Brook does the same. At this writing (1991) a large willow across the stream, about 1.75 mi from launch, necessitates a short carry. Shortly thereafter a dangerous strainer is just around a sharp bend to the right. Obviously, such obstacles may move from year to year.

Cheningo Creek enters L at about the 2-mi point. Its wide valley indicates that both of these streams were more vigorous in the geologic past. The low dam just above East River Crossing can be run at the center to the left of the island at M to H water. Stop and scout this; it involves at a minimum scratching the canoe. The remainder of the trip poses no great problem. There is moderate current at usual water levels, and there are some shallow spots.

Takeout The usual takeout point is Yaman Park in Cortland, which is reached by car by traveling I-81 to the Cortland exit and turning L on Rt 13. Immediately after passing under the I-81 bridge, turn R and drive down to the water's edge. The park is well marked by signs. A fee is charged in summer, when the canoeing is not very good anyway, but the rest of the year admission is free.

Tioughnioga River

County: Cortland

Segment ↕ Cortland to Marathon

Length ↔ 15 mi

Drop ↘ 80 ft

Difficulty ② Class II

Problems ✻ Strainers and sweepers; DO NOT RUN IN FLOOD!

Maps Cortland, McGraw, Marathon; DeLorme pp 47, 61

Contributor Ron Schlie

Launch Access is possible under just about any bridge that crosses the Tioughnioga. One good launch point is in Yaman Park, owned by the City of Cortland. This launch point is described in detail on p 54 (E. Branch, Truxton to Cortland).

Description The East Branch and the West Branch, which are described on the preceding pages, come together at Cortland to form the Tioughnioga River, (pronounced tie-uff-nee-oh-ga), locally called "the Ti." The Ti offers about 33 mi of very good canoeing between Cortland and Chenango Forks, where it joins the Chenango. At usual stages, it offers enough but not too much challenge to the average paddler and is deservedly popular.

Caution ✖ If the river appears to be over its banks and running through trees and over grass, it is in flood. The hydraulic power under these conditions has to be felt to be appreciated. An inexperienced canoeist can be caught under such conditions in a strainer and find it difficult if not impossible to extricate himself.

Cortland to Blodgett Mills: This section might be "scratchy" at times of low water; at other times it presents no great difficulty. The river is 30 to 40 yds wide at the start and gradually narrows. Watch for strainers in blind corners.

Blodgett Mills to Messengerville: The speed of the river picks up as the valley narrows. In this section small rapids will be encountered; the paddler should look for the vees.

Small islands will also be encountered; many canoeists experienced with the Tioughnioga feel that the east (L) channel is frequently the best, but the judgment of the paddler on the scene always takes precedence.

Messengerville to Marathon: Just after the bridge come two sharp turns in quick succession, with a short chute in the middle. Quick and skillful maneuvering is required here. To the W of the route is a large hill which keeps the river in shadow in the afternoon; to the E is a flood plain. This section also contains islands; the best route is the same as described in the paragraph above.

Takeout Just N of Marathon the river swings very close to Rt 11 near Osco Robinson Post # 617, American Legion. Do not park at the Post but across the street, where there is ample parking in a roadside pullover. Cars parked here can be seen from the river by the approaching canoeist, as can the Legion building.

Camping ▲ There are three commercial campgrounds in the general vicinity of Marathon, none of them very close to the river. They are Country Hills and Yogi's Deer Run, Marathon; and Upper Lisle Campground, Whitney Point.

Note ☞ A large Grumman plant at Marathon manufactures canoes and other aluminum boats.

Tioughnioga River

Counties: Cortland, Broome

Segment ↕ Marathon to mouth (Chenango Forks)

Length ↔ 19 mi

Drop ↘ 128 ft

Difficulty ① Class I

Problems Whirlpools and sandbars at mouth

Maps Marathon, Lisle, Whitney Point, Chenango Forks; DeLorme pp 47, 48

Contributors Charlie Murn, Mark Freeman, and others

Launch The recommended start for this trip is just N of Marathon on Rt 11 across from Osco Robinson Post # 617, American Legion. (See preceding entry.) Rt 11 hugs the east side of the Tioughnioga River from Cortland to Whitney Point, so any paddler desiring to leave the river can climb out and pull his canoe up to the road. Unfortunately, he may not find a legal parking space close at hand.

Description In contrast to its branches above Cortland, the Tioughnioga is a fair-sized river at Marathon and not surprisingly becomes larger before it empties into the Chenango at Chenango Forks. From Marathon to Whitney Point, Rts 11 and I-81 roughly parallel the route. The gently moving current is relaxing and interesting in any season, with the exception of the muddy floodtime usually associated with spring runoff. Carp can actually push a small canoe around as they rush for good spawning sites in the calmer water. The shoreline is covered with daffodils in late spring and ferns in summer; in May hillsides along the route are adorned with white trillium. There is adequate water at any time of year; although drought may make the going scratchy, the river comes up fast after a rain.

The river flows through fields in a fairly narrow and steep-sided valley, switching back and forth to hug the east and west slopes alternately. There are few if any impediments. About 3 mi from launch, Jennings Creek enters R, although its mouth may be hard to spot. Very shortly thereafter the bridge at the hamlet of Killawog is passed, and about 4 mi farther the Rt 79 bridge and the village of Lisle are reached. There is easy river access R under this bridge, and if the wind is S the paddler may well wish to end the trip here. It is necessary, however, to carry canoes several hundred yards (around a gate which prevents vehicle access) to available parking on a side street across from the Christian Fellowship Church. The building with a steeple, which is near the gate, is now a private home.

The mouth of the Otselic and the two bridges at Whitney Point are 2.5 mi from here. An official takeout beach with ample parking close to the river is R downstream from the second bridge, which is Rt 206. Many paddlers will choose to end their trip at Whitney Point to avoid the difficulties downstream. About 4 mi farther, the river passes under a small bridge at Itaska. On the R downstream from the bridge is a gaging station. Five miles from here, the Tioughnioga passes under Rt 12 and a RR bridge and reaches the Chenango. Turbulence, whirlpools, debris and sandbars mark the confluence of the two rivers.

Takeout Rt 79 parallels the river on the northeast from Whitney Point to Chenango Forks, intersecting Rt 12 just above the mouth of the Ti. A popular takeout point is about .5 mi above the Rt 12 bridge, where a small channel L of an island leads to an access point. The carry is up a short steep bank, then across a grassy field behind Charlotte Kenyon Elementary School, which can be seen from the river. Parking is usually possible in the school parking lot; when school is in session it is wise to obtain permission. It is also possible to take out L below this point, about 100 yds upstream of the bridge.

For another access point which has advantages and disadvantages, the canoeist can continue down the

Chenango River for about 1.5 miles to Chenango Valley State Park. The park has all the usual facilities, including camping, and would be a good spot for a week's camping while exploring the Chenango, Otselic, and Tioughnioga rivers, but takeout is difficult here even for those with camping permits and the park rangers discourage canoe access for those without. The park is on the east side of the river. The canoeist who wishes to exit the Chenango here must proceed through a labyrinth of channels and islands, hugging the true east bank. After passing the golf course, then woods, the route reaches the parking lot. Here a large culvert can be seen ahead. Fifty feet upstream of this culvert, which is the outlet of the park lake, a log blocks entrance to a natural cove, and canoes can be pulled up a short bank to the parking lot.

Otselic River

Counties: Cortland, Broome

Segment ↕ Cincinnatus to Upper Lisle

Length ↔ 15 mi

Drop ↘ 50 ft (depending on lake level at reservoir)

Difficulty ① Class I

Problems ✻ Gravel bars, chutes near end

Maps Cincinnatus, Willet; DeLorme p 47

Contributors ✍ Alice Broberg and Ron Schlie

Note ☞ Previous guides suggest that the Otselic River is canoeable for approximately 40 mi, from the village of Otselic to its junction with the Tioughnioga below Whitney Point, and that is certainly technically correct. However, this guide, ADK, and the Ka-Na-Wa-Ke Canoe Club do not recommend any stretch other than that described here for the following reasons: Above Cincinnatus, the river is not only fast but full of obstacles, including vicious strainers and frequent barbed wire. At M level or less, the current is much slower and the hazards consequently less, but canoes will have to be dragged through shallows. At the end of the recommended trip, it is possible to continue below Upper Lisle, paddle the entire lake (with its possible winds) and carry .5 mi around the dam, but it is hardly worth it for the short and relatively uninteresting 2-mi trip to the Tioughnioga.

Launch Take Rt 41 S and E from Cortland to the hamlet of Cincinnatus. Turn N on Rt 26, launch at more northerly of two bridges R off 26. Steps lead down to the river on the east side at a town park beside the fire house; there is good parking. Routes 41 and 26 parallel the stream on the west side as far as Willet, where both cross, 41 heading off E and 26 continuing down the river on the east side.

Description Unless there is a strong south wind, this trip is pleasant and easy. In early spring, caps and gloves are advisable, and no flowers will have appeared yet, except for some roadside coltsfoot. The trip may be made later as well, since this stretch maintains an adequate volume most of the summer. In July and August, however, it is apt to be scratchy in the first mile because of flood control grading done by the US Army Corps of Engineers, and at ML level the river is very shallow on and off for about .5 mi beginning at the 2-mi point. The stream flows under the second bridge at the .75-mi point and moves S in a straightforward way, hugging the steep hill to the W. A couple of islands offer a choice of channels. After 1 mi Brakel Creek enters L, and at the 3-mi point the river braids around several islands close together. For the next mile there are reverse curves, often with sweepers and strainers, which should not be attempted at H water levels.

About 5.5 mi from launch, Rts 26 and 41 cross the Otselic at Willet. The very popular access site here can be reached by car by doubling back on the old highway immediately after crossing this bridge toward the E. After the bridge, the paddler experiences a noisy riffle; then flatwater moving through a wooded corridor followed by an opportunity to practice maneuvering skills down some easy riffles and around wide turns. One or more strainers may also be encountered here. A gravel bar about 5 mi from Willet makes a good place to beach canoes and stop for lunch. Chewed alders and bank slides here testify to beaver activity.

About 11 mi from launch is the next bridge, Carr Rd off Rt 26 in the hamlet of Landers Corners. A state boat launch site is just downstream R. From this point on, the forested shoreline gradually gives way to clearings as the route approaches Whitney Point Wildlife Management Park. High cliffs ahead R signal the canoeist that the takeout point is just ahead. A sharp left turn through gravel bars, a small chute (depending on water level), lively riffles at a wide right turn, and a bridge end the trip.

Takeout There is a state boat launch site at the Wildlife Management Park, which has good parking and toilet facilities. It is reached via Rt 26 from Willet. Depending on wind conditions, paddlers may wish to continue about 3 mi down Whitney Point Lake to Dorchester Park, a Broome County public park with all of the usual facilities except overnight camping.

Note ☞ In April 1991 the bridge from Upper Lisle across the river was out, making it much more practical to end the trip at

Landers Corners or to paddle down the lake to Dorchester Park. It is not known when this bridge will be back in service.

Camping ▲ Upper Lisle Campground, mailing address Whitney Point, is a commercial campground very near the river. It is across the no-longer-usable bridge from Upper Lisle but can be reached by a detour through Landers Corners.

Mark Freeman

A once-perfect canoe after a trip down the Otselic River . . . Noone was hurt and the canoe has since been mended.

Allegheny Watershed
Part II

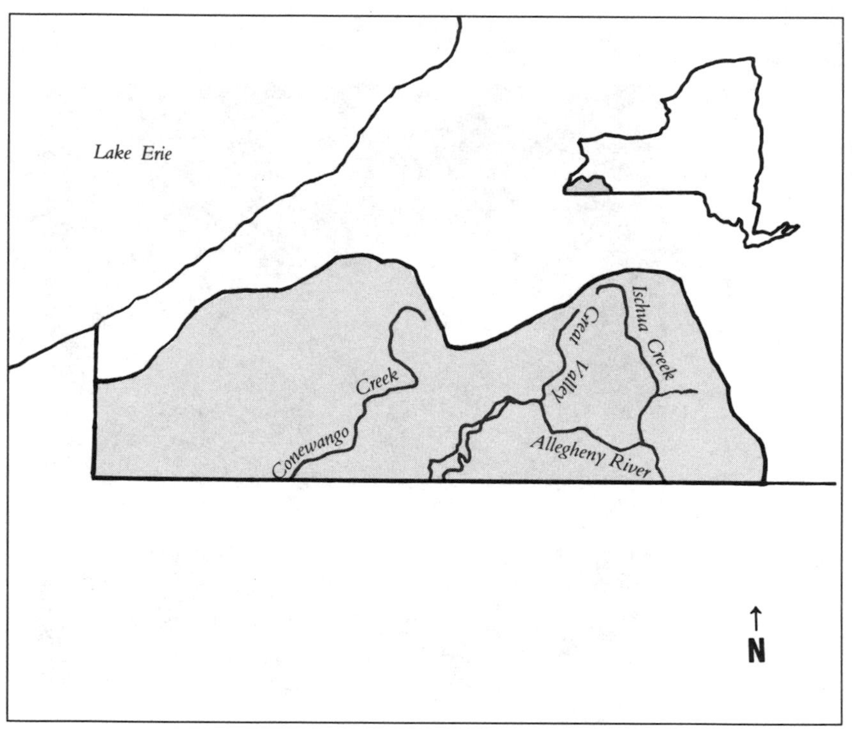

Allegheny River

County: Cattaraugus

Segment ↕ Vandalia to Kill Buck

Length ↔ 12 mi

Drop ↘ 20 ft

Difficulty ① Class I

Problems ✻ None

Maps Knapp Creek, Limestone, Salamanca; DeLorme p 41

Contributor Joe Ginett

Launch Access is possible at most bridges. Suggested launch for this trip is at the only bridge in Vandalia, which connects Rts 417 and 60, 3 mi E of the point at which Rt 219 turns sharply S from 417. Access is at the south end of the bridge. Parking is available at the side of the road. Launch is also possible at the next bridge upstream, 4.25 mi away, but the first part of the trip would then be through a more urban setting.

Description The Allegheny River, which flows past the town of Allegany, is somewhat like the Susquehanna in reverse. The Susquehanna rises in New York, makes a loop into Pennsylvania, then comes back into our state before flowing through Pennsylvania and Maryland a long way to Chesapeake Bay. The Allegheny rises in Pennsylvania and makes a loop through New York before departing for Pittsburgh. Eventually its waters reach the Gulf of Mexico. At one time, steamboats are said to have ascended the river as far as Olean.

Allegheny River • Vandalia to Kill Buck

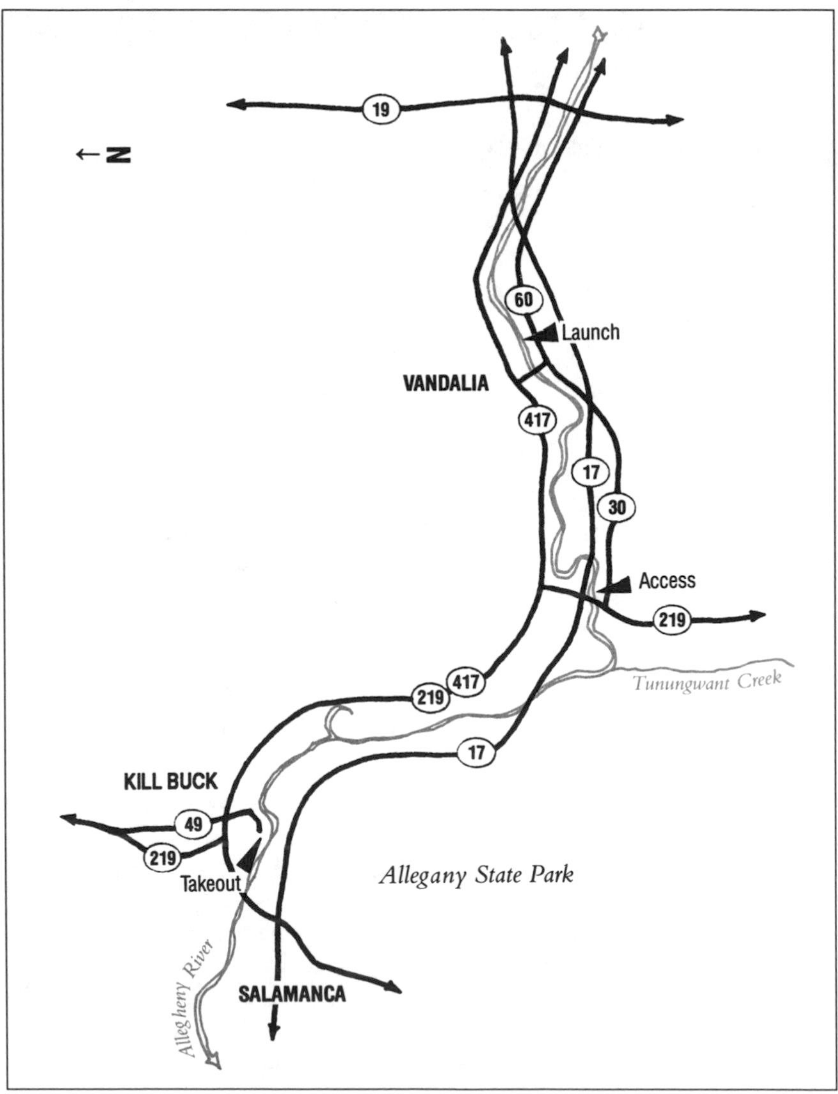

The 51 mi of the river in New York are all quite similar to the trip described here: wide pleasant flatwater with a little current. Much of the scenery is fairly urban or industrial; this is the oil-producing part of New York. About 3 mi past Kill Buck, the Allegheny Reservoir, the result of damming in Pennyslvania, begins, and what little current there was ceases.

This is a good trip for novices at M or lower levels and is not much more difficult at H. The water level is seldom too low for canoeing at this point, the river is wide, the turns are gradual, and the current gentle. While the river closely follows Rt 17, the paddler often feels far from civilization. The entire trip is within the confines of the Allegany Indian Reservation. It is necessary to obtain a permit to fish within the reservation, but canoeing has never been a problem.

About 4 mi from launch, the river passes under the Rt 219 bridge; access is possible here on the south side. At the 5.5-mi point, Tunungwant Creek enters from the S. The tributary is a substantial creek at this point, canoeable but not very interesting, winding as it does among oil wells. At this point the Allegheny turns rather sharply N. At the 9.5-mi point there is a large oxbow; the main channel is L. Two miles from here the end of the trip is reached, at the village of Kill Buck, just E of Salamanca.

Takeout Access is possible on river R in Kill Buck. Rt 49 in Kill Buck, or its extension, continues S across the RR tracks and turns to parallel the river. Canoeists can park here or on the street (near houses) N of the tracks.

Camping Allegany State Park is 5 mi SW of Salamanca and offers all park facilities.

Ischua Creek

County: Cattaraugus

Segment ↕ Rt 98 to mouth (junction with Oil Creek)

Length ↔ 17 mi

Drop ↘ 115 ft

Difficulty ① Class I

Problems ✲ Obstructions, sharp bends, mild rapids

Maps Franklinville, Hinsdale; DeLorme p 42

Contributors ✍ Beth and Dave Buckley

Launch Rt 16 parallels Ischua Creek for its entire length, providing convenient access at many points. The old grade of the Pennsylvania RR also parallels the stream. The creek is a Public Fishing Stream, and access is provided through landowner cooperation at many points. The uppermost possible launch point, the start of this trip, is where Rt 98 crosses Ischua Creek, 1.1 mi S of Franklinville. Access is downstream on river L. Parking is on road shoulder away from the bridge itself.

Description Ischua Creek rises in the hills W of Machias; its headwaters are now dammed up. It flows S to meet Oil Creek about 20 mi as the crow flies, not as the river runs, from its source. At the confluence, the two become Olean Creek. The trip described comprises flatwater, riffles, and light rapids, perhaps reaching Class I. Stream width is 10-15 yds. At less than M water level, the trip is difficult and probably not worthwhile. The first section is attractive open woodland and pasture, generally appropriate for novice paddlers with a bit of moving water experience.

Immediately after launch, Gates Creek enters L, nearly doubling the amount of water in the stream. This first section is serpentine and relatively sluggish. At the 3-mi point Ischua Creek passes under Coal Chutes Rd, and at 4.25 mi under Pierce Hill Rd. One mile farther is the Five Mile Road (Cty Rt 19) bridge.

Many paddlers prefer to launch here and take out at Farwell Rd rather than paddle the entire route. Access is L downstream from the bridge. With enough water, this section can be exhilarating. The hills crowd the streambed here and the current is livelier. There are enough light rapids to practice eddy turns and other maneuvers. Passing close to the hillside behind the village of Ischua, the stream scoots under a couple of interesting old bridges. Then it bounces back and forth across the narrow valley several times. Meadows and willow trees alternate along the banks. Just before the Farwell Rd access point is some very old stonework that is said to be the 200-year-old remains of a canal, never completed, intended to go up the valley from the Allegheny River. The Farwell Rd bridge is about 3 mi S of Ischua, just off Rt 16.

It is 3.75 mi from here to the junction with Oil Creek, for those who wish to paddle the entire stream. The valley opens up, and neither the scenery nor the fastwater is particularly interesting. The route passes under a couple of small bridges and, just before the confluence, the impressive twin bridges of Rt 17, a major expressway.

Takeout A very short distance after Ischua and Oil creeks join to become Olean Creek, a state boat launch site R offers good access and parking. It is reached from Rt 16 by driving W across the bridge at Hinsdale.

Camping Valley View, Ischua, a commercial campground, is on the left bank of Ischua Creek about 1 mi S of Five Mile Road.

Great Valley Creek

County: Cattaraugus

Segment Ashford to second Rt 219 bridge, N of Salamanca

Length 13 mi

Drop 200 ft

Difficulty Class I

Problems Possible strainers, sharp bends, one low dam

Maps Ashford, Ellicottville, Salamanca; DeLorme p 41

Contributors Beth and Dave Buckley

Launch Just S of Ashford, N.Y., Devereaux Branch and Beaver Meadow Creek flow together to form Great Valley Creek. Launch here into Beaver Meadow Creek on river L downstream of the Rt 242 bridge. The launch point is reached by taking Rt 219 N 8 mi to the Rt 242 junction in Ellicottville, then continuing straight on 242 when the two separate. The bridge is about 4 mi farther. Parking along the road is possible.

Description This stream is ideal for novice or intermediate outings; novices should be accompanied by at least a few more experienced paddlers. While the gradient is fairly steep, it is remarkably uniform throughout the run, and this stream is runnable by less than expert paddlers when other creeks may be too high for safe paddling. The creek is not runnable below MH water level. It is fastwater and riffles all the way, with no real rapids. There may be strainers, but in May 1991 there were none in evidence, nor were there any fences.

Immediately after launch, the paddler enters Great Valley Creek proper and turns R downstream. The route passes under Rt 242 twice in the first 2 mi. Deer and wild turkeys may be seen, and trout swim in the stream. The first 5 mi are the most attractive, passing through farmland and forest. Paddlers can practice backferrying and eddy turns; the stream is small enough to allow one to step out of the canoe and correct maneuvering errors. A low dam is just downstream of Ellicottville. First-timers should scout this R and decide whether to run it or carry around, based on water level and their own skills. A strong eddy at the base of the dam makes the relaunch quite tricky.

Slightly over 5 mi from launch is the Brewer Rd bridge off Cty Rt 71, 2 mi S of Ellicottville, where some choose to end the trip. Parking is on the shoulder of the road. Above this point Cty Rt 71 parallels the stream L. The creek moves in a fairly wide, steep-sided valley with surprisingly few meanders. After the route passes under a minor bridge, Forks Creek enters L at the 10-mi point, adding considerably more water; Wrights Creek, 12.5 mi from launch, is a carbon copy. Between the two, Rt 219 passes overhead at the village of Great Valley, and the stream goes under it again at mi 13, just N of the junction of Cty Rt 49 (Kill Buck Rd) and 219.

Takeout 13 mi from launch, just downstream from the second Rt 219 bridge, access is possible R. Vehicles should be parked off the shoulder on the west side of Rt 219 well away from the bridge railings. Canoeing below here is not recommended. Those who wish to paddle the entire creek to its mouth will have 3 mi of uninteresting semiurban scenery below this point, followed by a difficult takeout.

Camping ▲ Allegany State Park is 5 mi SW of Salamanca and offers all park facilities.

Conewango Creek

County: Chautauqua

Segment ↕ Waterboro to Frewsburg

Length ↔ 16 mi

Drop ↘ 20 ft

Difficulty ① Class I

Problems ✻ None

Maps Kennedy, Ivory, Jamestown; DeLorme p 40

Contributors ✍ Robert Rogers, Beth and Dave Buckley

Launch Highest recommended launch point is at the Rt 394 bridge E of Waterboro. This is reached by taking Rt 62 S from Buffalo or N from Jamestown to the intersection with 394 and turning E on 394 1.25 mi to the bridge. Parking is available just off Rt 394 at E end of bridge. Access is through a private drive to a small creek that quickly joins the Conewango; permission must be obtained. Considerate use will probably mean that permission continues to be granted. Alternate access is possible at several bridges along the route. Chautauqua County maintains several access points at town roads along the route.

Description Conewango Creek rises in southwestern Cattaraugus County and flows S and somewhat W until it leaves New York just W of Fentonville. It flows into the Allegheny at Warren, Pennsylvania. Its upper reaches are often marshy and are ditched for miles in places. It offers pleasant if not very exciting canoeing for 18 mi or more, especially at H levels. Flowing between fairly low banks, it offers a good view of woodland, and waterfowl, deer, and muskrat may be seen. Some of its most attractive features are the riffles for several miles below launch.

About 2.5 miles from launch, the first Rt 62 bridge is reached, and at the 5-mi point the creek flows under Rt 17, a major expressway. One mile from here the Cty Rt 42 bridge is reached. A state launch site, a popular access point with plenty of parking, is here. It is reachable by driving W .5 mi from 62 at the hamlet of Clark. Nine mi from launch the stream flows under Hartson Rd. About 2 mi farther Cassadaga Creek enters R in a confusion of channels and islands. Dolloff Rd bridge is also at this point. Below here the stream turns W, flowing under Rt 55 N of Frewsburg, then S to reach Rt 62 .75 mi W of Frewsburg.

Takeout Most canoeists will elect to take out at the second Rt 62 bridge. There is ample parking here. It is possible to canoe another 5 mi to a state launch site W of Fentonville. This site is on a large loop in the creek just before it flows into Pennsylvania.

Camping Chautauqua County maintains a lean-to campsite on an island (at least at high water) near the state launch site. The island is the site of an abandoned town, most of which has been obliterated by periodic high water.

Lake Erie Watershed
Part III

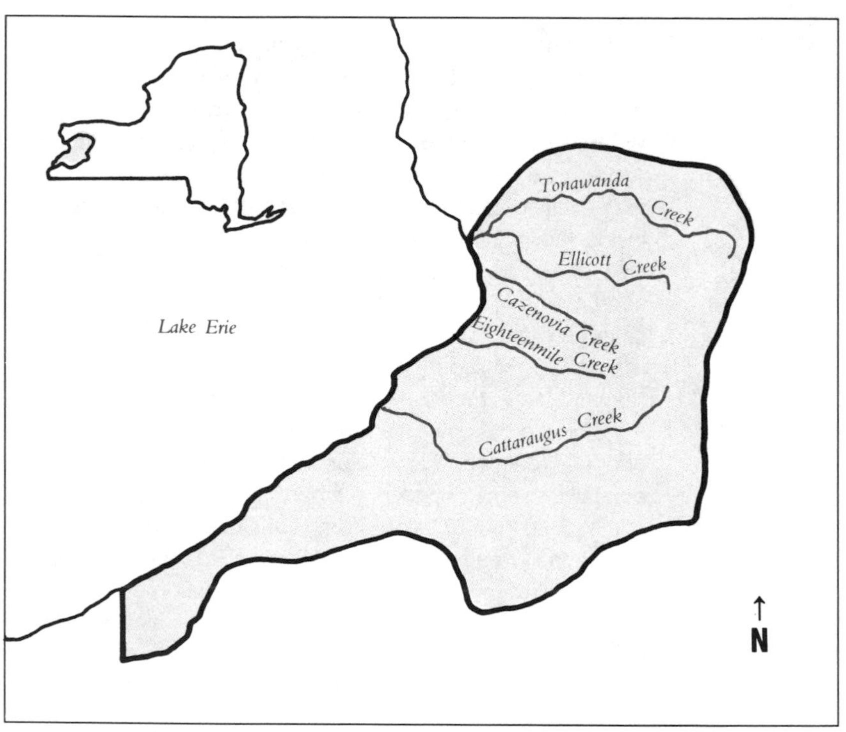

Cattaraugus Creek

Counties: Cattaraugus, Erie

Segment Rt 16 to Scoby Rd (Springville Dam)

Length 18.5 mi

Drop 260 ft

Difficulty Class II

Problems Rapids, gravel bars, sharp turns, possible down trees; dam to be portaged

Maps Arcade, Sardinia, Springville, W. Valley, Ashford Hollow; DeLorme pp 56, 55, 41 (NOTE: Paddlers can probably dispense with Springville and W. Valley quadrants; in all, about .5 mi of the creek is on the two together.)

Contributors Daan Zwick, Beth and Dave Buckley

Launch Rt 39 generally follows Cattaraugus Creek from Arcade to just E of Springville; most access points are reached from this route. The Rt 16 bridge is a good launch point except at L water levels. It is reached by taking 39 W from Arcade 2.5 mi to where it intersects 16 and turns N with it. The bridge is .25 mi N of this intersection; access is upstream of the bridge on the north side of the stream. There is adequate parking nearby.

Description Cattaraugus Creek rises in the hills of Wyoming County, very close to the source of Tonawanda Creek. It flows S a few miles, then turns W to parallel Tonawanda, which flows N and then turns W. The two creeks form the northern and southern boundaries of Erie County for most of their length, until Cattaraugus empties into Lake Erie and Tonawanda into the Niagara River, the lake's outlet. Cattaraugus is generally considered to provide the best whitewater paddling in western New York.

The section above Springville Dam flows through eroded farmland over a sand and gravel bottom. At MH or higher levels this can be an uninterrupted fast run until the slack water above the dam is reached. The stream has many twists and turns where the eroding banks have built up gravel bars. In the first 3 mi the stream drops 90 ft, a very steep gradient. Although there are no ledges or boulders, the canoeist must have the skills to deal with sudden obstacles, such as down trees, and quick changes of direction. About 3 mi from launch Elton Creek enters L. A popular alternative launch site is where Stone Quarry Rd (the extension of McKinistry Rd) crosses this tributary less than a mile above the confluence.

Most of the run is on moderate current through open pasture and woodland. Below Elton Creek the gradient gradually decreases throughout the trip; in the last 5 mi above the dam the stream drops only 50 ft. At the 8-mi point, the stream flows under Hake's Bridge (W. Townline Rd), which is just off Rt 39 about .5 mi E of Van Slyke Rd. This is a popular access point, often used as a starting point by paddlers who prefer somewhat less challenge than is found above it. There are still occasional obstructions and sharp bends that deserve a cautious approach. In particular, a seemingly permanent collection of logs under a RR bridge just downstream of here requires a cautious approach. The few moments it takes to land and walk the canoe around a tricky spot can actually save time as well as possible trouble.

Bigelow Bridge (Rt 240) is 12 mi from Rt 16, and Felton Bridge at Edie's Siding is 15.5. (NOTE: DeLorme and the USGS disagree as to where this hamlet is; the USGS is

Cattaraugus Creek • Rt 16 to Scoby Rd (Springville Dam)

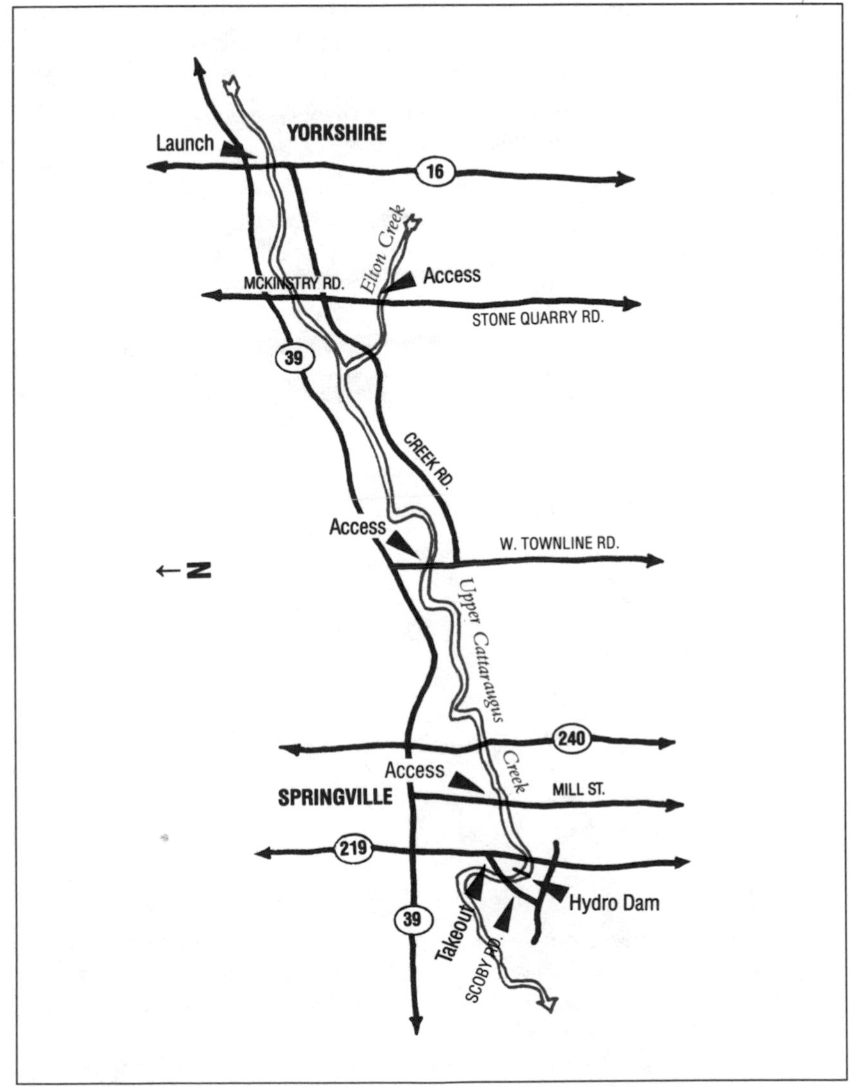

correct.) Buttermilk Creek enters L just before the second bridge. US 219 crosses the stream just before the end of the trip. About .5 mi below the US 219 bridge is Springville Dam. The steep portage is R; about .25 mi below the dam is Scoby Rd bridge.

Takeout Access to the creek is on the north side by Scoby Rd bridge. Scoby Rd deviates SW from US 219 about 1.5 mi N of the 219 bridge. After loading or unloading boats, drivers should move cars back to the main road.

Cattaraugus Creek

Counties: Cattaraugus, Erie

Segment Scoby Rd to Zoar Bridge ("Burt's")

Length 11 mi

Drop 100 ft

Difficulty Class II

Problems Rapids, down trees

Maps Ashford Hollow, Collins Center; DeLorme p 41

Contributors Daan Zwick, Beth and Dave Buckley

Launch Put in at Scoby Rd. (See previous entry.)

Description This is not unlike the previous section, a relatively uninterrupted run, with but one bridge to pass under. It is classified II at H water levels because of haystacks and the need to maneuver quickly around them if in an open boat; there is a similar need to maneuver around fallen trees jutting out from the bank in the wooded stretches.

Immediately after launch, it is necessary to get to the middle of the stream to avoid rocks near the right bank. The stream flows through the scenic Zoar Valley; Zoar Valley Rd parallels its course R. Just below Frye Bridge (Hammond Hill Rd), 4.25 mi from launch, Connoisarauley Creek enters L. Below here the gradient steepens, although the rapids never exceed Class II. Deer, ducks, and even beaver may be seen as the setting grows increasingly wilder.

Takeout The abandoned Zoar Bridge, in the area known to whitewater paddlers as "Burt's" because a small refreshment stand by that name was formerly located there, is visible ahead on a straight stretch; a state access site is L before the bridge. Zoar Bridge is reached by following Zoar Valley Rd W about 7.5 mi from US 219. Zoar Valley Rd intersects 219 about 1 mi S of Rt 39. The bridge, the second one reached, will be obviously barricaded to vehicles; at most water levels it is necessary to land L and carry boats and gear across the bridge to the north side. Vehicles must not be left immediately N of the barricade but may be parked along Zoar Valley Rd.

Caution The stretch of water below this point is Class III, possibly Class IV at higher water levels. It should not be attempted in an open canoe at very high levels, nor in any craft, at any water level, by paddlers without good whitewater skills and proper equipment. Three boats is generally regarded as the minimum number to attempt this next trip. Current is very fast over shallow shale ledges. Scouting some drops is difficult and time-consuming but essential. There is no access between this point and Gowanda without extreme difficulty; the stream flows between the sheer unclimbable walls of a gorge. A swim here is likely to be a very unpleasant experience.

Cattaraugus Creek

Counties: Cattaraugus, Erie

Segment ↕ Zoar Bridge ("Burt's") to Versailles

Length ↔ 15 mi

Drop ↘ 290 ft

Difficulty ③ Class III verging on Class IV at H and higher levels

Problems ✻ Ledges, rapids, haystacks, ice falls in early spring

Maps Collins Center, Gowanda, N. Collins; DeLorme p 41, 40, 54

Contributors ✍ Beth and Dave Buckley, Daan Zwick

Launch Access to this stretch is at the bridge at Burt's. (See previous entry. Be sure to read carefully the CAUTION.)

Gauge The levels at the bridge at Burt's are painted on the concrete foundation on the south side. Below 1.5 is too low; 2.0 to 2.5 is ideal for open boats; only experts who are familiar with the river should run this stretch in an open boat at 3.0 or above. A highly skilled and experienced paddler says this: "(My wife) and I live within ten minutes of the Cattaraugus. We don't run it in open boats above 3 ft. Period. At higher levels an upset could easily lead to injury or damage to canoes."

Description Arguably the best whitewater stretch in western New York, this is not for beginners at any time, nor for intermediates except in warm weather at relatively low water (1.5 ft on the gauge at Burt's). For much of the route, the cliffs of the Zoar Valley Gorge are unscaleable. Boats should have plenty of flotation, and wet suits are a must, except when the water and air are quite warm. In addition, the canoeist or kayaker may encounter commercial raft trips.

One surprising characteristic of this difficult run is its relatively tame beginning. The first 2 mi are straight and uneventful, giving the canoeist a chance to enjoy the gradually rising cliffs as the gorge is entered. As the Zoar Valley Gorge closes in, the Cattaraugus takes on the aspect of a wilderness river. The stream meanders; there are riffles and Class I rapids. In early spring, there may be masses of ice hanging on the south wall; the paddler must stay in the center of the stream to avoid falling ice. About 2 mi into the gorge, a bridal-veil waterfall tumbles two or three hundred feet down the cliff on the north. About 4 mi from Burt's the cliffs are some 400 ft above the river, and for much of the rest of the trip the rugged shale walls of the gorge support almost no vegetation.

Soon after this point, the rapids become Class II to III, with angling ledge-drops and cross currents and standing waves guaranteed to keep most paddlers' minds off the scenery. Just above the confluence of the South Branch are two large holes, one on the far right and one on the center left. The best place to run this stretch is on the far left. These hydraulics have been known to flip large rafts. The confluence, about 5.5 mi from launch, is a good lunch stop. There is an emergency takeout L .3 mi below the confluence, but it involves a long, steep carry out to a dirt road running N from Point Peter Rd.

From this point on, rapids are all II to III, or higher. It is advisable to stop and scout at many points; consider lining down if conditions look too difficult. Even experts who have previously made this trip always scout Tannery Rapids, the trip's whitewater climax at mile 9, just before Gowanda. This rapids begins a few hundred yards below the long concrete retaining wall of a factory building on the south bank. It should be scouted L and can be carried L if conditions warrant. Some paddlers believe lining down this rapids R is easier and safer than carrying L. Above the 4-ft level, the carry is under fast-moving water. The railroad bridge, which can be seen from a distance, crosses the stream about a hundred yards below the end of the most difficult stretch of Tannery Rapids. The rapids can also be scouted from this bridge after cars have been parked in Gowanda, before the run, for the eventual takeout.

Those who want only the challenge of the rapids usually take out in Gowanda, 150 ft below the highway bridge in the center of town, on the R. It is important not to block the access of fire trucks to the river at this point. Parking is available nearby; this is the back of a shopping center.

The stretch to Versailles ("Versales") is a fast, pretty run of just over 5 mi between wooded banks. The route passes through the Cattaraugus Indian Reservation. While the gradient is only slightly less than the previous stretch, rapids are less difficult because there are no ledges, only occasional boulders, and the stream is generally straighter, with fewer eddies. At lower water levels, there is a ledgy rapid under the bridge that could be rough on hard-hulled canoes.

Takeout The first bridge after Gowanda is at Versailles. It provides access to the stream L, the exact location depending on water level. This is the center of town; owners of various nearby buildings usually grant permission to park when it is requested.

Note ☞ It is possible to canoe another 11 mi from Versailles to Lake Erie. The trip is much like the stretch from Gowanda to Versailles, but the gradient gradually decreases. The last 5 mi is flat, slow, muddy, and unattractive. The route continues through the Indian Reservation; there is no bridge for the first

8 mi. Fishing, especially for salmon, is said to be good here, but a permit is required to fish within the reservation.

Eighteenmile Creek

County: Erie

Segment Hamburg to Lake Erie

Length 11.25 mi

Drop 185 ft

Difficulty Class III

Problems 2 broken dams, an 8-ft falls, rapids, possible large waves at mouth

Maps Hamburg, Eden; DeLorme pp 54, 55

Contributors Kent Iggulden, Doug Bushnell

Launch Hamburg can be reached via I-90, Exit 57. There are several possible launch points in Hamburg. The farthest upstream is at the parking lot across the street from Saints Peter and Paul Roman Catholic Church, 66 E. Main St, Hamburg. It is usually possible for canoeists to park here. Launch is down a long grassy hill; the edge of the stream here is lined with protective riprap. At MH or lower water level it is necessary to launch farther downstream. A second possible access is just below the bridge on S. Buffalo St. Parking is available in the vicinity. A third launch point in this area is just outside the village of Hamburg on Rt 62 (which is also US 75 at this point) at a public area near the Water Valley Restaurant, which is popular with canoeists.

Description Eighteenmile Creek rises in the hills near Springville, N.Y., and flows roughly NW to Hamburg, then W to its mouth at Highland-on-the-Lake, Lake Erie. Canoeing above Hamburg is not recommended by this guide, although it is done by expert and daring kayakers at time of very high water. It is said to approach Class V.

The trip described, very popular with whitewater enthusiasts, especially kayakers, is only for skilled paddlers with proper equipment, in groups. There are some areas with high cliffs that would make rescue difficult. Water levels are unpredictable, since the watershed is quite small; adequate water in the morning may be history by afternoon. This trip has been made successfully in open canoes, by experts, at less than flood level.

Launch to Rt 62, 1.75 mi: Between the recommended launch and the E. Eden bridge are a couple of good surfing waves at H water levels. About 500 ft below the E. Eden bridge is a 2-ft high concrete dam with a 3-ft wide hole in the middle. This dam, at the village park on Woodview Ave, has never been a problem and almost seems to disappear at H water levels. It can be scouted by taking out R. At this writing there is a large broken willow tree at the dam R. There are no other hazards in this section, just a few more good surfing waves.

Rt 62 to S. Creek Rd, 1.5 mi: Just below the Rt 62 access is the first of two major hazards to be found on this trip: an old mill dam, almost completely broken away. This can be scouted from the Rt 62 bridge or access point. The largest remaining section of the dam is L. Center is a large pillar, and R is a concrete section about half the size of the left section. There may be a log or logs as well. After scouting, the paddler may decide to line down, carry around, or run the gap, perhaps taking advantage of the eddy behind the pillar. Below the opening is a large shallow flat rock area that ends with a haystack and must be avoided. Just downstream, the route passes under a RR bridge; from here to S. Creek Rd are numerous play waves.

S. Creek Rd to Versailles Rd, 4.5 mi: The S. Creek Rd bridge is easily recognizable from the stream because it is the newest bridge on the route.

Caution ✖ Just below this bridge, the stream makes a sharp left turn and drops over an 8-ft waterfall. According to local historians, there was once a mill here; what appears to be an old canal is cut through the shale wall L. This falls is runnable but must be scouted first.

Takeout is possible L at the end of a large shale cliff. There are usually no obstructions at the foot of the falls, but fallen trees are always possible. At this writing, there is a fallen tree completely blocking the creek 1.5 mi below the falls. It can be portaged R and may be gone tomorrow.

About 2.75 mi from S. Creek Rd bridge is the confluence of the main stream and the South Branch. From here on there is enough water for canoeing, even at M levels. Launch is possible just below the confluence from North Creek Rd, which parallels the stream on the right at this point. Halfway between the confluence and the US 20 bridge is Pine Tree Rapid, Class III, which is very popular with kayakers. About 1 mi farther the route passes under the twin bridges of I-90 and then the US 20 bridge.

Note ☞ Takeout is not possible at any of these bridges, but .5 mi below the US 20 bridge is a bridge closed to traffic, at the end of Versailles Rd, and takeout is possible here just below the bridge R. Canoes must be carried across the bridge and to the nearest public parking, near the post office in the hamlet of N. Evans, at the corner of S. Creek Rd and Versailles Rd. This is a short distance by car W of the US 20 bridge.

Versailles Rd to Lake Erie, 3 mi: There are a few play waves in this section, but no very challenging rapids. About

.75 mi from Versailles Rd, there are twin RR overpasses to paddle through. At the 2.3 mi mark, it is possible to take out R just past the Rt 5 bridge, but it is necessary to carry canoes up out of a gorge over rocks covered with wire to halt erosion. There is a small public parking area at the corner of Rt 5 and Stanton Rd. From here, it is .75 mi of mostly flat water to Lake Erie, passing under the old Lake Shore Rd about halfway. This bridge is painted bright blue and at this writing is closed to vehicular traffic.

Note ☞ The residential area between Rt 5 and Lake Shore Rd is completely posted, with numerous "No Parking" signs. Under no circumstances attempt to land or park in this area.

Takeout It is possible to take out at the old Lake Shore Rd bridge, which at this writing is being replaced by a new bridge. Since there is no legal parking here, it is necessary to park at the corner of Rt 5 and Stanton Rd and carry boats approximately .15 mi. An alternative for canoeists who are not too tired at this point, if wind has not raised waves on the lake, is to paddle 4.5 mi SW to a state launch site at Sturgeon Point.

Caution ✖ Like all large lakes, Lake Erie can be very rough. If there is a likelihood of wind from NE to SW, the trip should be ended before emerging onto the lake.

Cazenovia Creek

County: Erie

Segment ↕ Tannery Rd (W. Falls) to Mill Rd (E. Seneca)

Length ↔ 18 mi

Drop ↘ 250 ft

Difficulty ② Class II, possibly Class III at very high water

Problems Small falls, rapids, possible down trees

Maps Colden, Orchard Park; DeLorme p 55

Contributors Michael Ford, Beth and Dave Buckley

Launch The recommended access point, Tannery Rd bridge, is reached by turning S from US 20A onto Davis Rd (Cty Rt 240) about halfway between E. Aurora and Orchard Park. At the village of Jewettville, 5 mi from 20A, Tannery Rd goes E .5 mi to the bridge over Cazenovia Creek. Launch should be upstream of the bridge to avoid offending local residents, and river L to avoid paddling too close to shale cliffs. Parking is possible on the right side of the road just before the bridge.

Description The East Branch and West Branch of Cazenovia Creek join near E. Aurora, forming a stream which eventually flows through downtown Buffalo and into Lake Erie. This trip begins on the West Branch and continues on the main stream after the confluence. Cazenovia Creek, a very scenic stream, runs for the most part between shale cliffs 100 ft high. It is the closest whitewater run to the Buffalo area. The first section described is only canoeable at MH to HH levels, while the stretch from Willardshire Rd to Mill Rd may be done at M water. The East Branch is not generally considered canoeable, nor is the West Branch above Tannery Rd; canoeing below Mill Rd is not recommended because of the slower current and urban development. Most rapids on this trip are Class I, perhaps Class II at HH level; a few are Class II at any runnable level and possibly III at HH; at least at that level they are deserving of great respect. A pleasantly fast current makes 6 hrs about average for the 18-mi trip.

Tannery Rd to Willardshire Rd, 9 mi: This section is narrow in places; trees may partially or totally block the stream. These can usually be seen ahead but can be dangerous at H levels; they should be given a wide berth. Rapids and fastwater begin immediately. A half mile below launch, under the Jewettville Rd bridge, is a slate outcrop, a 2-ft ledge across the stream. This is the most difficult drop in this section, but it can be run, the center being probably the best route. It can be scouted from under the bridge on the L, and may be lined down R fairly close to the right bridge abutment. For someone on this creek for the first time at H level, the problem is seeing the ledge in time to exit and line down, if desired. The Jewettville Rd bridge is the key.

The next few rapids are Class I, or possibly II at H level. About 2 mi farther, the route passes under Taylorshire Rd, and under Holmwood Rd 1 mi after that. The East Branch enters R .5 mi farther; very shortly thereafter the creek goes under Rt 20A (Big Tree Rd). At this point the stream does a 180; the paddler who was traveling E a few minutes ago now finds himself facing W. About 4 mi farther, the stream bends N, then NE, and the Willardshire Rd bridge can be seen ahead. The trip may be broken here; access is possible R just before the bridge. This point is reached by car by driving N from US 20A or S from US 20 on Transit Rd to Mile Strip Rd. Mile Strip Rd is 2.5 mi N of 20A; it intersects Willardshire .4 mi E of Transit. Willardshire continues .8 mi SE to the bridge.

Willardshire Rd to Mill Rd, 9 mi: This section is more open and the creek is wider, but the current still moves right along, with frequent riffles and some Class I rapids. Just before the Northrup Rd bridge, 4 mi into this segment, the stream turns gradually E and then sharply W. Looking ahead, the paddler can see slack water and a clear horizon, the usual signs of a dam. This time, however, it's a falls, a 3-

to 5-ft drop. There is an easy portage R. After scouting, the falls may also be run; the easiest route is on the extreme L where there is a steep narrow chute with a 3-ft drop. Cautious or non-expert canoeists may elect the portage. This is a possible access point; Northrup Rd goes NE from Transit Rd .5 mi S of the US 20 intersection. The bridge is 1.25 mi from Transit Rd. Some rock gardens near the Transit Rd (US 20) bridge, 1 mi farther, require careful maneuvering. From this point on, the trip involves only riffles and fast water to the Mill Rd bridge.

Takeout Mill Rd is a right turn off Seneca St .3 mi E of Union Rd (Cy Rt 277). The bridge is .25 mi from the intersection. From the river, takeout is R just before the bridge. There is a parking lot here.

Tonawanda Creek

Counties: Genesee, Wyoming

Segment ↕ Varysburg to Batavia

Length ↔ 25 mi

Drop ↘ About 200 ft, 150 in first 9 mi

Difficulty ① Class I

Problems ✻ 2 dams

Maps Attica, Alexander, Batavia S; DeLorme p 56

Contributor Daan Zwick

Launch Rt 98 parallels the stream throughout this stretch, crossing from E to W about two-thirds of the way from Varysburg to

Attica. Access points are easily reachable from this highway. Launch is at the Rt 20A bridge in Varysburg, a village about 6 mi S of Attica. Parking, with permission, is possible at one of the commercial establishments in the vicinity.

Description Tonawanda Creek rises in the hills of Wyoming County and flows N to Batavia. Here it turns W, meandering through an Indian Reservation of the same name, becoming the boundary between Erie and Niagara counties and finally emptying into the Niagara River at N. Tonawanda. It is not canoeable above Varysburg and only canoeable from here at H water level.

Varysburg to Attica, 9 mi. Shallows and deeper stretches alternate to a ford and abandoned bridge at Eck Rd at the 2.5-mi point. From here to the bridge at Cotton Hill Rd and on to the Rt 98 bridge, the 6-mi point, there are a few riffles and more deep water. More meandering and fewer riffles lead to the Dunbar Rd bridge, followed by deeper water to the dam at Attica.

Caution ✖ While it is possible (at water levels that make the trip from Varysburg feasible) to run the sloping dam and the flat rock stream bed below it, it should be done carefully and only after scouting. It can be scouted from a spot behind the firehouse. If the rapids are not to be run, a good takeout point is on the east bank under the RR bridge; it is convenient to a parking lot behind a bank on Main St, Attica.

Attica to Batavia, 16 mi. After taking out at the RR bridge or dam, a car shuttle is necessary to get to the launch at the Prospect St bridge (if the short rapids below the dam do not appear to be runnable). This bridge is reached by turning E off Rt 98 about 1 mi N of the traffic light in Attica, just N of a small shopping center. The launch is upstream of the bridge on the west bank. There is plenty of parking nearby.

As the grade decreases, the stream has fewer shallows and meanders a bit but still has an appreciable current.

Farmland and small wooded areas predominate on the way to Alexander. There is one bridge (Stroh Rd) in this 5-mi section. It is a clear run under the bridge in the center of Alexander and under the new Rt 20 bridge just beyond. North of Alexander the gradient decreases and the stream winds more slowly through a very wide valley. Most of the land is scrub woods and wetlands, with almost no houses or roads visible. Some bridges shown on USGS or other maps no longer exist; the only presently existing bridge between Rt 20 and Batavia, the Peavner Rd bridge, is not shown. There may be an occasional log jam to haul over or carry around. The stream deepens and slows, with many meanders, as it approaches the large dam in Batavia. Two RR bridges and a water tower on the right bank signal that the paddler is approaching the dam.

Takeout It is possible to take out on the west bank just below the Ellicott St bridge beyond the two RR bridges. There is also a later takeout, on the east bank just above the dam, next to the water tower. There is good parking here, accessible from nearby Main St.

Tonawanda Creek

County: Genesee

Segment ↕ Batavia to N. Pembroke

Length ↔ 12 mi

Drop ↘ 45 ft

Difficulty ① Class I

Problems ✱ Possible down trees

Maps Batavia S, Batavia N, Oakfield, Corfu/Alexander (7.5 x 15); DeLorme pp 70, 56

Contributor Daan Zwick

Launch Access is below the dam in Batavia. (See previous entry.)

Description At Batavia, Tonawanda Creek makes a series of gentle left turns; from here to the Niagara River it flows generally W rather than N. In spite of its name, it is a good-sized river from here on. Wide, slow, and sometimes meandering stretches are punctuated by falls and rapids which are frequently not canoeable.

About .5 mi from launch the route passes under a bridge on the west side of town; the road connects W. Main St (Rt 5) with S. Main St. Four miles farther the creek turns N and passes under Rt 5. This stretch has meanders and oxbows; Creek Rd parallels the stream to the N. At about the 6.5-mi point, the creek makes a big dip to the S; one-half mile farther Bowen Creek enters L. Shortly after this the route passes under two local road bridges in the vicinity of E. Pembroke. Turning N again, the creek passes under the twin bridges of I-90 at the 9.5-mi point. About 1 mi farther, paddlers will encounter a small dam just before the takeout. This should be scouted and possibly carried, but it is broken out R and can be fairly easily run at most water levels.

Takeout Just below the dam L at the Maple St bridge in N. Pembroke is a convenient access point. Parking is possible on the shoulder of the road. This spot is reached by car by taking Rt 5 from Batavia W about 6 mi to E. Pembroke, turning N on Read Rd and crossing the creek. After passing over I-90, Read Rd or its extension intersects Maple St 1.25 mi from E. Pembroke. The access point is .5 mi N of this intersection.

Note ☞ The next recommended access point is at Rt 93, N of Akron. Between Maple St and Rt 93 various problems make canoeing difficult if not impossible. At Indian Falls, 2 mi beyond Maple St, the creek drops well over 125 ft in less than 2 mi. High and muddy banks make access impossible in many places. This area is in the Tonawanda Indian Reservation. Some places that look like access points on maps are not legal or public, and many bridges that appear on maps to be usable are in reality barricaded.

Tonawanda Creek

Counties: Niagara, Erie

Segment Rt 93 to Wendelville

Length 24 mi

Drop 15 ft

Difficulty Class I

Problems None

Maps Wolcottsville, Clarence Ctr, Tonawanda E; DeLorme p 69

Contributor Daan Zwick

Launch Access to this stretch of the creek is almost never easy (see previous entry). It is possible, however, to launch at the Rt 93 (Wolcottsville Rd) bridge, 5 mi N of Akron. Parking is feasible S of the bridge on the W side where the shoulder appears to have been made wider for that purpose. The access point is under the bridge and is muddy, but it is less muddy at higher water levels.

Description With a gradient of under 1 ft per mi, Tonawanda Creek provides a less-than-thrilling ride from here to the point at which it becomes the Barge Canal, but it does offer novice paddling, with occasional riffles, in a rural setting. Beaver are often seen here. Even at relatively H levels, the current is not so strong as to be especially difficult for tandem paddlers going upstream, and round trips are possible.

About 1.25 mi from launch, Ledge Creek enters L, carrying with it the waters of Murder Creek, whose source near Attica is only a few hundred yards from Tonawanda Creek. All of these creeks meander endlessly in this area; in some stretches Tonawanda takes more than 10 mi to cover an airline distance of less than 5. At the 5.5-mi point, the creek passes under a small bridge connecting Block Church Rd with Tonawanda Creek Rd; there is no access here. (For the rest of this trip, the road parallel to the stream on one side or the other, sometimes both, is called Tonawanda Creek Rd.)

About 10 mi from launch, the Rapids Rd bridge is reached, and 5 mi farther the creek passes the village of Rapids. There are no discernible rapids in Rapids, and no one in the village knows why it is called that, although there is a place where the stream widens and becomes shallower. Access is possible at the bridge in Rapids.

Below Rapids the stream takes a somewhat more direct course. It is a pleasant run with a mixture of woods and cottages on the banks. The Rt 78 bridge near Millersport is 20 mi from launch; W of that bridge there is a paved bicycle path on the south bank. One-half mile farther, Mud Creek enters R, and 1.25 mi beyond is the New Rd bridge, after which the creek merges with the Erie Canal.

Takeout Two miles farther on the south bank, just after Ransom Creek enters L, is a public access area with plenty of convenient parking and a relatively shallow bank with a choice of takeout spots. It is reached by taking the Rt 78 exit on I-90, driving N about 9 mi to Millersport, and turning W onto the (S.) Tonawanda Creek Rd. for about 4 mi.

Ellicott Creek

County: Erie

Segment ↕ Bowmansville to mouth at Tonawanda Creek

Length ↔ 16 mi

Drop ↘ 125 ft (much of this is at Glen Falls)

Difficulty ① Class I

Problems ✻ One large waterfall, numerous strainers around blind corners

Maps Lancaster (7.5 x 15), Buffalo NE, Tonawanda E; DeLorme pp 55, 69

Contributor ✍ Lynn Mancuso

Launch This trip begins at the Genesee St bridge in Bowmansville. Roadside parking is available, and additional parking is possible at a firehall parking lot a short distance N of this bridge. Many will prefer to skip the first 2.5 mi and launch at Greater Buffalo International Airport, at Aero Drive just off Youngs Rd, where plenty of off-road parking is available.

Description ✏ Ellicott Creek, like Olean Creek, has no source under its own name. It is formed where Crooked Creek and Elevenmile Creek come together NE of Alden, N.Y. At M or higher water levels it offers attractive canoeing in a mostly pastoral setting a few miles from the heart of downtown Buffalo, but the trip is best at H level. Canoeing above Genesee St is mostly through swamps, but there is a small but dangerous falls just above this recommended launch point.

The creek winds past islands and through every type of landscape: back yards, commercial property, RR tracks, and woodlands and meadows with mallards and great blue herons. Because of sharp turns, strainers appear suddenly. Scouting is recommended, and portages may be necessary. After about 2.5 mi, Ellicott Creek disappears into culverts under a runway of Buffalo International Airport.

Caution ✖ Takeout is mandatory before this point and is possible at Aero Drive near Sugg Rd. There is sufficient roadside parking here. Canoeing through any of the culverts would be very dangerous and perhaps impossible. They turn and twist, and no clear line of sight is possible. Aero Drive also passes through a tunnel under the runway; a vehicular portage is recommended. Walking through the dimly-lighted tunnel on the narrow walkway and carrying a canoe in the face of heavy truck traffic would be as hazardous as canoeing a culvert.

About .5 mi from the relaunch on the other side of the tunnel described above, the creek passes under I-90. The scenery is a mixture of residential backyards and fields. About 1 mi from launch is an island. The left channel is usually better, although it, too, may be blocked with down trees. Beyond this point the paddler may see hawks, ducks, woodchucks and other wildlife.

Extreme Caution ✖ Glen Falls, a 3-story drop, is about .5 to .75 mi from this point. The canoeist should familiarize himself in advance with the takeout and carry around this hazard. The takeout is in the Village of Williamsville in the Town of Amherst at Island Park, which ceases to be an island at lower water levels and is therefore difficult to recognize. There is NO exit below Island Park, but sheer rock walls on either side. The takeout is L from the main stream onto the "island." A footbridge ahead serves as a warning; *take out before this bridge.* Carry off the island crossing the wide footbridge L (not the same footbridge mentioned in the previous sentence). From here the carry on foot passes between the library and the town office building and turns R on Main St, then L into the entrance to Glen Park. The carry continues downhill along the river, past the falls to Glen Ave. Here a bridge R crosses the creek; E of the bridge is a bike stand and the path to the launch 100 ft downstream. It is also possible to make this carry by car. There is a public parking lot behind the town offices and another beside the bike stand, and Rock Ave leads from Main St to Glen Ave. It is of course possible to begin the trip below the falls and avoid this hazard completely.

Below the falls, the creek winds through woods, fields, and country clubs. Paddlers may observe yellow finches, an occasional great blue heron, and wildflowers, but they should also watch for tricky bends, tree branches, and footbridges. Numerous small islands enhance the scenery. Less than 2 mi from relaunch, Sheridan Drive is reached. This is a possible takeout point for those with no time to go further. The Church of Our Savior parking lot is on river right here; permission should be obtained before parking. It is also possible to park on Indian Trail Rd. A canoeist who lives nearby says of this part of the route: "This part is the most beautiful; however, in recent years it has become increasingly dangerous. The creek can become very swift and makes sudden blind turns. During storms, old trees have fallen to create dangerous strainers; last year I got caught in one of these and my life was endangered. This year (1991),

Ellicott Creek: Glen Falls

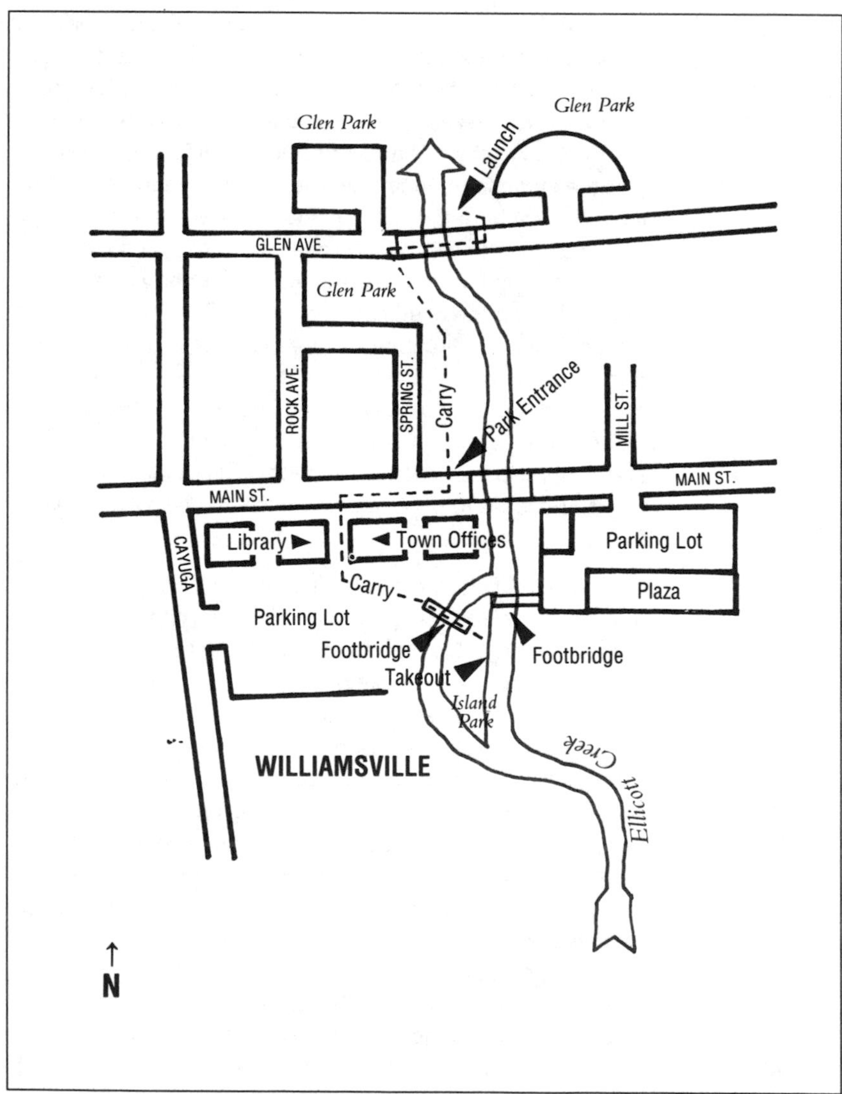

I walked the entire section before I paddled it." At this writing, there is one very large strainer (about .67 mi from relaunch) that necessitates a portage.

Below Sheridan Drive the creek widens. After less than a mile, the sewage disposal plant is passed R. One-half mi farther, the paddler encounters an odd-looking and somewhat intimidating Army Corps of Engineers weir at Maple Rd. The creek first is diverted into a wide, shallow, but canoeable pond, then becomes narrowly constricted between walls. The resultant increase in current offers no threat; in fact, the whole area is fun to negotiate. Below this point, golf courses and meadows continue, and the paddler may see deer as well as small animals and birds. Three mi below Sheridan Drive, the creek passes under Rt 263. It may be choked with debris under this bridge. Just beyond here, at the U. of Buffalo campus, the paddler may encounter a very aggressive pair of Canadian Geese that returns each year. If they have a brood, it is best to give them as wide a berth as possible and pass speedily. The most pleasant part of the trip ends 2 mi farther.

Takeout There is good access R at N. Forest Rd, just about where I-990, a conspicuous landmark, crosses Ellicott Creek, and easy parking at a bend in the road. It is possible to canoe another 6 mi to Tonawanda Creek without any particular difficulty, but the scenery becomes more urban and commercial. At the mouth of Ellicott Creek, the canoeist may turn W down the barge canal (Tonawanda Creek) .25 mi to the Niagara River, then N downstream .75 mi to a boat launch site in the center of North Tonawanda opposite Tonawanda Island.

Lake Ontario Drainage, Western Part
Part IV

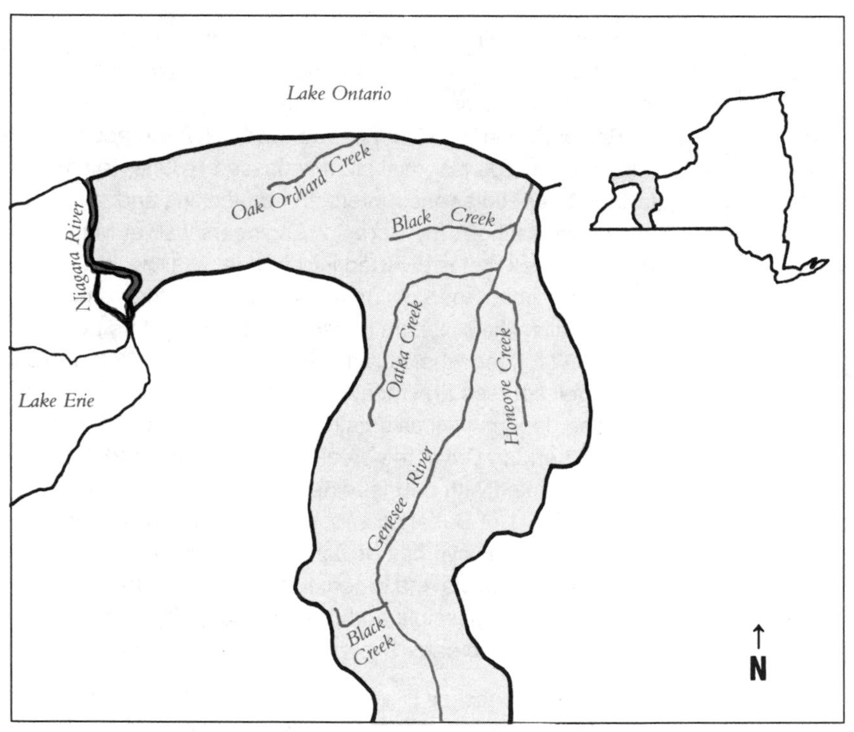

Niagara River

County: Niagara

Segment ↕ Lewiston to Fort Niagara

Length ↔ 7 mi

Drop ↘ Negligible

Difficulty ① Class I

Problems ✻ Sizable waves from wind or motorboat traffic; strong eddies at south end

Maps Fort Niagara, Lewiston; DeLorme, p 68

Contributor Robert Rogers

Launch Access is readily available at Lewiston Landing, the village boat launch site. It is reached by turning W off Center St onto Water St and continuing a short distance to the end. Parking facilities are good here. Lewiston is 7.5 mi N of the city of Niagara Falls on I-190.

Description The boundary between New York and Ontario at this point, the large and powerful Niagara River, is after its awesome display at Niagara Falls quite canoeable for its final 7 mi. At the launch point and above, under the Lewiston Bridge, strong eddies may astonish the paddler by hurling him *upstream* at 5 mph. Because of the waves and the current this is not a spot for a beginner, but intermediate or better paddlers will enjoy it. The scenery is beautiful, with New York State and Ontario Provincial parks on either hand. There is always a more-than-adequate flow, making this an attractive midsummer paddle.

Takeout There is a boat launch ramp in Fort Niagara State Park, where the Niagara River empties into Lake Ontario. Fort Niagara is reached by driving 6 mi N from Lewiston on Robert Moses Parkway.

Note This is an entirely feasible and pleasant 14-mi round trip for a pair of strong paddlers or a single kayaker. It would be difficult for a solo canoeist. Going upstream, current may be minimized by hugging the American (E) shore.

Caution Because of the powerful currents and treacherous eddy lines, paddlers should not venture very far upstream from Lewiston.

Oak Orchard Creek

County: Orleans

Segment Rt 63 S of Ridgeway to mouth (Lake Ontario)

Length 20 mi

Drop 140 ft (80 at dam)

Difficulty Class I

Problems Possible fallen trees, waves on lake when windy

Maps Lyndonville, Ashwood; DeLorme p 70

Contributor Daan Zwick

Launch Oak Orchard Creek is very close to the east side of Rt 63 1 mi S of Ridgeway. Launch is easy from the level stream bank here, and parking is available on the wide road shoulder. By car, this spot is reached by leaving I-90 at the

Batavia Exit, going S into Batavia and taking Rt 63 N and W through Medina to the site, which is 3 mi N of Medina.

Description Oak Orchard Creek rises just N of Batavia, many miles N of the launch site, but its upper reaches are lost in a maze of swamps and canals. (It is one of the feeders of the Barge Canal.) It is not generally paddled above the recommended launch point; although it is possible to launch at a bridge a short distance upstream, parking is not good there. Large waterfalls at Medina are also a deterrent. The portion described is an excellent introduction to moving stream paddling for beginners; the skills practiced in the first couple of miles can be put to good use on the rest of the trip. It is canoeable at M water level or higher. The shallower water is below the Rt 104 bridge.

At the launch, the stream is slow-moving with easy curves. The banks are farmland but soon become wooded. At the 1-mi point the creek flows under Horan Rd, after which the current gradually increases, but the bottom remains sandy. The Bates Rd bridge comes at the 2-mi point; now the current increases further and an occasional rock protrudes, or doesn't quite. This portion of the creek is forced to flow E by The Ridge, which geologists say is the shoreline of an ancient lake. Five miles from launch a break in the geological structure allows the stream to turn N. At this point it flows under Rt 104 (Ridge Rd); access is possible here.

After turning N the stream changes character, becoming wider, shallower, and rockier. Here the skills acquired on the upper section can be put to use avoiding rocks. An occasional miss (that is, a hit) is more embarrassing than dangerous, since the current is still not very fast.

About 8 mi from launch Carlton Yates Town Line Rd crosses, and a short distance farther the slack water of Lake

Alice is in evidence. Those who do not wish to paddle flatwater can exit here R, landing on the flat just above the bridge and carrying up the bank to the road. Parking is possible on either side of the road just E of the bridge, which is 1.5 mi N of the intersection of Carlton Yates Town Line Rd and Rt 104.

Lake Alice, 5 mi long, is formed by the high Niagara Mohawk power dam near Waterport. Its greatest width is .5 mi, but it is often narrower, and it is bridged at Kenyonville and Waterport. Strong north and east winds can make this part of the trip difficult. The dam, 1 mi beyond Waterport, can be carried R down a steep bank.

Below here Oak Orchard Creek soon reaches lake level; it has little current after the initial run just below the dam. This lower portion, about 6 mi long, is crowded with marinas, fishing boats, and other power craft. The trip ends at Lake Ontario.

Takeout Oak Orchard State Marine Park is L at the mouth of the creek and has the usual launch and parking facilities. It is about 1 mi N of the Oak Orchard Exit of Lake Ontario State Parkway. After exiting, drivers must cross the creek and go N to the end of the road.

Camping Lakeside Beach State Park is about 2 mi W of the takeout; Wildwood Lake Family Campground, Medina, is a commercial campground a few miles NW of the launch site.

Genesee River

County: Allegany

Segment Shongo to Belmont

Length 22 mi (5 mi skipped)

Drop 200 ft (dam at Wellsville skipped)

Difficulty ② Class II, some stretches possibly Class III

Problems ✲ Dam at Belmont, log jams S of Wellsville, often at sharp bends; a powerful stream at flood level

Maps Wellsville S, Wellsville N, Belmont; DeLorme p 43

Contributor Daan Zwick

Launch Rt 19 parallels the Genesee for this stretch; most access points are reached from that route. The southernmost launch point on the Genesee in New York is the Rt 19 bridge at Shongo. This is a public access point with parking. This section of description starts with a launch here.

Note ☞ At H or MH levels, experienced paddlers could start at Genesee, Pa., 3 river miles upstream. NY Rt 19 becomes PA Rt 449. The access point is at a bridge just E of the first intersection at the north end of Genesee, where 449 turns S.

Description The longest river in western New York and the third longest in the state, the Genesee is one of the few major streams in the US to flow N. It rises in the mountains of Pennsylvania and empties into Lake Ontario at Rochester. It is the only river which flows from the southern boundary of the state to the northern boundary, and thus the only major stream which intersects the Barge Canal. About 300 ft of its 1400-ft drop occurs in the three major falls and other rapids in Letchworth State Park. (See p 113.)

Shongo to Jack Bridge, 7 mi: At launch, the stream is clear and fast-running, with wooded banks. This stretch is not for beginners; at the H water level needed to run it, the current is strong. There are sharp bends, with down trees waiting just around the corner to snare the unwary or inexperienced. One mi from launch, Graves Rd crosses, offering another good access point, R, upstream of the bridge. Although some banks in this stretch are posted, there is a state-maintained parking lot here, and good banks for easy access. Graves Rd runs W from Rt 19 about 1 mi N of Shongo. The stream is braided, with numerous small islands, and good river judgment is needed to pick the best route.

Several smaller streams join the Genesee in the vicinity of the Mapes Rd bridge, about 3 mi farther, so this can become a starting point if the water is too low for a start farther upstream. Mapes Rd (Cty Rt 29) runs W from Rt 19 at York Corners, about 5 mi S of Wellsville. Three mi farther, an excellent takeout or lunch spot is the public fishing access at Jack Bridge Rd, which has parking and picnic tables. Beyond Jack Bridge the banks are less friendly, and there is no access at Weidrich Road bridge, 2 mi farther. There is also the potential problem of a small dam 1 mi beyond that, at the southern boundary of Wellsville. The 2 mi through Wellsville have been constricted into a diked channel. For all these reasons, it is probably better to carry by car from Jack Bridge to the Rt 417 bridge at the north end of Wellsville.

Rt 417 to Belmont Dam, 10 mi: Launch at the west end of the Rt 417 bridge, just N of the bridge, near the sewage treatment plant and airport. USGS Wellsville N quadrant makes life more difficult by labeling Rt 417 as Rt 17, which was perhaps true in earlier days but isn't now.

From here, with the addition of several tributaries including the large Dyke Creek in Wellsville, the Genesee is definitely a river, big and sometimes meandering, traveling through a partly agricultural, partly wooded, wide and

Genesee River • Shongo to Jack Bridge

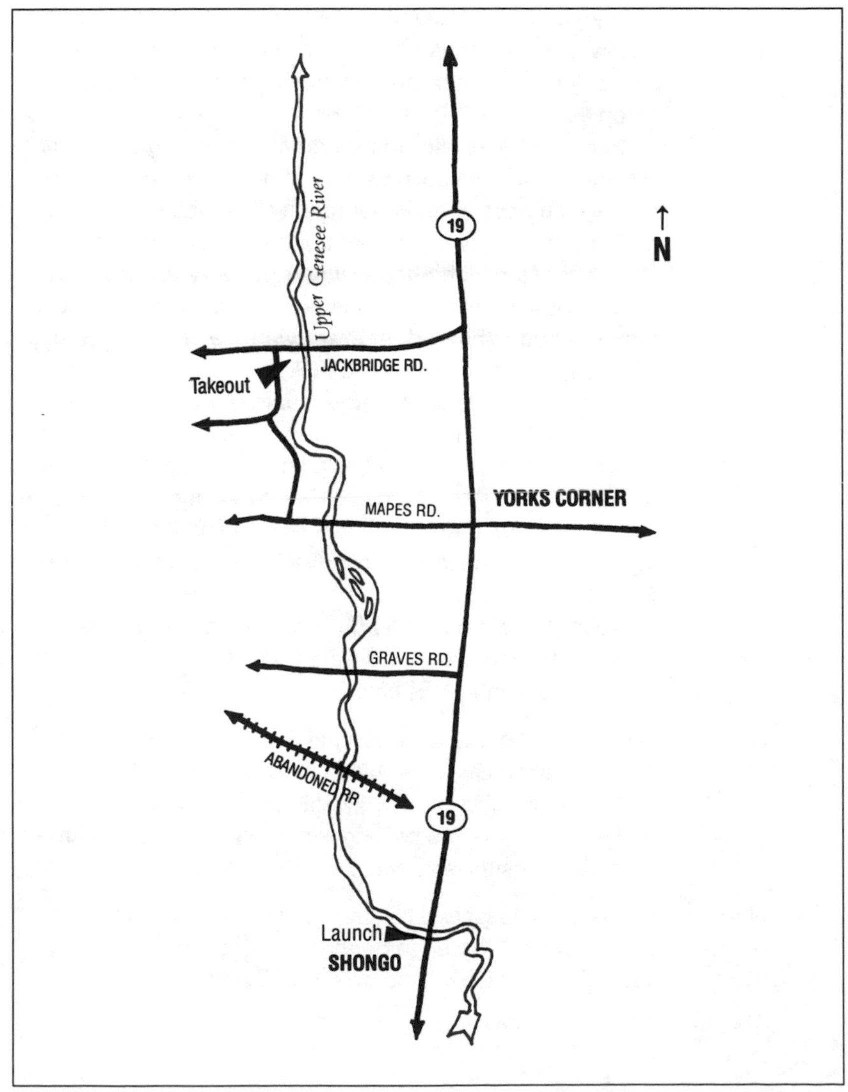

not very steep-sided valley. There are even a few cut-off oxbow lakes. Because of the erosion from changing river levels, the banks can be very muddy and sometimes steep.

Between Wellsville and Belmont at H or higher levels smooth stretches alternate with short, shallower, faster runs which occasionally approach Class II difficulty. The rapids are easily visible from upstream; the runs are straightforward with choppy water but very few real haystacks. Down trees on the inside of bends probably pose a more serious hazard. At lower water levels, the paddler must be able to maneuver to pick the best channel to avoid getting hung up on gravel bars or bumping rocks.

County Rt 9 (Knight Creek Rd) crosses the river at Scio, about 4 mi from launch. At this point, there is public access with parking on the west bank. Five mi farther, at Cty Rt 31A (Corbin Hill Rd), there is a town park with parking, picnicking, and toilet facilities. Both of these county routes intersect Rt 19 E of the river.

About 1.5 mi from 31A, the large dam at Belmont is reached. Paddlers should be alert. There are several channels; hug the right (NE) bank.

Takeout On the right bank, just above the dam, access is feasible. Rt 19 crosses the Genesee just at this point; regular on-street parking is possible on Rt 19 just N of the west end of the bridge. On weekends parking is possible with permission at commercial establishments E of the bridge.

Camping ▲ There are at least two commercial campgrounds in this area: North Hill Camp in Shongo (mailing address Wellsville) and Park Meadows, E of Belmont.

Genesee River

County: Allegany

Segment ↕ Belmont to Caneadea

Length ↔ 19 mi

Drop ↘ 125 ft

Difficulty ① Class I, Class II in the vicinity of Belfast,especially at H level

Problems ✻ Rapids above Belfast

Maps Belmont, Angelica, Black Creek, Houghton; DeLorme pp 42, 43

Contributor ✍ Daan Zwick

Launch (See previous entry.) There are two options for launch below the dam at Belmont. One is to carry directly across Rt 19 to the firehouse and launch from the right bank there. The other is to carry across the bridge to the left bank, where there is a small stairway down to the river. Water level will determine which choice is easier.

Description The 19 mi from here to Caneadea can be a clear run at M or higher water level and is runnable at any level except the lowest. It is not a trip for a group of beginners but is suitable for paddlers with a slight amount of experience accompanied by more skilled canoeists. The skills required vary with water level; at higher levels many hazards are buried, but it is necessary to be able to cope with a powerful current and strong eddies and ferry away from down trees. At lower levels the paddler needs to be able to stay in the deeper channel and avoid hitting rocks. Scouting from bridges while placing cars for shuttle should provide sufficient information to experienced canoeists.

The best route through the short Class II rapids just downstream of launch can be scouted from the bridge. Van Campen Creek, L about 3 mi from launch, adds a good deal of water to the Genesee. About 1.5 mi farther at Belvidere there is excellent access, with a boat launch and parking on the west (L) bank, at the Cty Rt 20 (Gibson Hill Rd) bridge. Gibson Hill Rd intersects Rt 19 at Belvidere; the access is NE of town. Just beyond the Gibson Hill Rd bridge is the much larger Rt 17 bridge.

In the next 10 mi, from Belvidere to Belfast, the Genesee meanders more, making wide, sweeping loops in a wide valley; the gradient is only about 5 ft per mi. Just after Angelica Creek enters R, the Transit Hill Rd bridge is a landmark halfway through this stretch. Black Creek enters L 4 mi farther. (See p 122.) At Belfast there is good access with parking on the east bank just before the Cty Rt 26 bridge, which is reached by driving E .5 mi from Rt 19 in the center of Belfast. From here the current picks up for the 5 mi to Caneadea, with a drop closer to 10 ft per mi. At Oramel, about halfway, the piers of an abandoned bridge are not difficult to avoid.

Takeout Cty Rt 46 crosses the Genesee at Caneadea and reaches Rt 19 in the center of town, about .25 mi farther. Takeout is not difficult on the east bank just before the bridge, where there are launching and parking facilities.

Genesee River

Counties: Allegany, Wyoming, Livingston

Segment ↕ Caneadea to Whiskey Bridge

Length ↔ 21 mi

Drop ↘ 120 ft

Difficulty ① Class I (Class II at H water level)

Problems ✻ Log jams probable N of Fillmore and elsewhere, small rapids

Maps Houghton, Fillmore, Portageville; DeLorme pp 42, 43, 57

Contributor ✍ Daan Zwick

Launch Access is at Cty Rt 46 bridge at Caneadea. (See previous entry.)

Description This run is not as difficult as the two preceding, but it does have several fast stretches, some small rapids, and the possibility of down trees, log jams, and strainers. The river meanders in a nearly mile-wide flood plain between steep hills E and a RR embankment W. In places the oxbows have formed islands and the paddler must choose the best channel. There are few bridges or intermediate access points on the route. Except for the Harland Hale bridge at Shongo Valley Rd, just N of Caneadea, there is no crossing for the first 10 mi, until Fillmore is reached. (The Lattice Bridge N of Houghton, shown on many maps, is barricaded.) Just above Caneadea the river is augmented by Caneadea Creek, which is dammed about 3 mi upstream to form Lake Rushford, which has picnic and swimming areas.

When the river veers to the E at Houghton, the buildings of Houghton College can be seen on the hill to the W. About 2 mi beyond Houghton the wide flood plain ends and the river flows more directly NE to Fillmore. Approximately 1 mi from this point, the canoeist encounters a small Class II rapids which is easy to see from upstream, just before the valley opens out again S of Fillmore. Just S of the Cty Rt 4 bridge, at Fillmore, there is good access on the west bank, but the firmness of the parking area should be checked before driving onto it in wet weather. This bridge is reached by going E at the traffic light in Fillmore. At this intersection, where Cty 4 intersects Rt 19, 19 turns sharply W.

From here to Portageville, 19A parallels the river on the west (L) bank. About .5 mi N of Fillmore there seems to be a perennial log jam, and others may be encountered on this stretch. In May 1991, the river had made an obvious channel around this jam. The 5 mi from Fillmore to the interestingly named Wiscoy Creek are fairly easy paddling otherwise. The river is wide and fairly straight, with no serious rapids but enough current to keep the boat moving right along. Wiscoy is a corruption of West Koy; the creek is joined by East Koy Creek shortly before it enters the river. It is a well-known trout stream. From Wiscoy Creek to Whiskey Bridge is 8 mi. The river winds more in this stretch, and there are some islands, but the paddling is fairly straightforward. Slightly less than a mile before Whiskey Bridge the steep hills to the east drop back and the first farm fields for some time are seen. At this point there may be a large log jam that should be scouted L.

Takeout Conclude this portion of the Genesee River at Whiskey Bridge, about 13 mi N of Fillmore. Whiskey Bridge, a relatively new, high-level bridge, is the first bridge across the river below Fillmore. Access is on the west bank, just at the bridge. Although the old RR bed up above prevents direct access to Rt 19, what is left of an old road that once serviced the former, lower bridge ascends gradually to the S, reaching Rt 19 about .25 mi S of the new bridge. This provides easy vehicle access to the river bank and parking there. This very minor road is the first turn over the RR bed S of Whiskey Bridge.

Whiskey may be a further corruption of Wiscoy, but a more romantic story current in the area is that near the east end of the bridge years ago was an illicit still. If it were still there, it would be illicit still.

Note ☞ It is possible to canoe beyond Whiskey Bridge to Portageville, but this guide does NOT recommend it. If the landing were missed, the canoeist would probably go over the huge Upper Falls.

Camping ▲ Hickory Lake is a commercial campground in the town of Houghton. At Letchworth State Park, just N of Portageville, camping is permitted and cabins are available.

Genesee River (Letchworth Gorge)

Counties: Livingston, Wyoming

Segment ↕ Lee's Landing (below Lower Falls) to St Helena

Length ↔ 6 mi

Drop ↘ 90 ft

Difficulty ③ Class III, except Class II at low water

Problems ✱ Long carry down and up steep banks, rapids

Maps Portageville, Nunda; DeLorme p 57

Contributors ✍ Ardie Shaffer and Daan Zwick

Note ☞ A permit from the park administration is required for access here. There must be at least three people in at least three kayaks or two canoes, and no one under 12 is allowed to run the river. It is necessary to telephone (716) 493-2611 for the permit, preferably two days in advance. Letchworth State Park, mailing address Castile, stretches along the river roughly from Portageville to Mt. Morris, which is 2 mi W of I-390 on Rt 408. Park Rd runs the entire length of the park on the west side of the gorge. All access points are reached from Park Rd.

Launch The trip starts at Lee's Landing, below Lower Falls, about .5 mi E of the park office on the west side of the river. Parking is at the top of the bank, after which paddlers must carry about 400 yds; the river is 110 ft below the parking lot.

Description Except for the long steep carries, this is a fun run in fast, clean water at the bottom of a steep gorge. Open boats require experienced paddlers at all but L water; extra flotation will make recovery easier. The river bottom has some sand, lots of gravel, and some rocks. Each of the three or four major rapids is less than 100 yds long, with a fairly quiet pool for recovery below. At H levels the paddler can choose among channels around gravel islands; at lower water the best channel will be obvious. In most cases, stopping and scouting is feasible, and the river width often provides a choice of more and less challenging routes through rapids.

Even in dry years this stretch is canoeable every fall for two to three weeks, when the Genesee "mysteriously" rises as Rushford Lake, upstream of Letchworth Gorge, is drained about the end of September. This is also the time of peak foliage color.

For the first mile from launch the course is N; then it turns W. At mi 2 the first rapid is entered. The only channel at L water (as well as the most challenging haystacks at H level) is to the right. After the pool at the bottom of this run, the river turns almost S and enters another rapid. A succession of relatively smooth runs, with sheer rock walls seemingly straight ahead, follows, then another rapid with pool and another big bend in the river. The top of the gorge here, 400 ft up, is less than a half mile wide.

Suddenly, about 5 mi from launch, the gorge widens, the river cuts through what is almost a flood plain, and the large flat area that once was the hamlet of St. Helena appears L. Ahead can be seen the piers of a long-abandoned bridge.

Takeout Land L upstream of the piers. Follow a track W across the flat; at the hill bear L and follow traces of a road .25 mi up to the St. Helena picnic and parking area, about 150 ft above the river.

Note ☞ Canoeists must report to the park office at the end of the run. All of the usual facilities, including camping and cabins for rent, are available in the park.

Caution ✖ Except for the trip described above, canoeing or kayaking is forbidden or not recommended between Whiskey Bridge (see preceding entry) and the dam at Mt. Morris (see subsequent entry).

Genesee River

County: Livingston

Segment ↕ Mt. Morris to Avon

Length ↔ 28 mi

Drop ↘ 41 ft (30 in first mile)

Difficulty ① Class I (Class II first mile)

Problems ✻ Rapids first mile

Maps Mt. Morris, Sonyea, Geneseo, Caledonia; DeLorme p 57

Contributor ✍ Daan Zwick

Launch Access is below the dam at the Rt 36 bridge N of the center of Mt. Morris. Since the riverbank here is often used for dumping it is necessary to search out the easiest and pleasantest spot to get down the bank to the river. Parking is possible at the little shopping center SE of the bridge. Mt. Morris is 2 mi W of the I-390 interchange with Rt 408.

Note While at less than flood stage this is not a difficult trip after the first drop (or with launch at Rt 20A), 28 mi can be a long day trip, which will seem longer because of the many meanders. Paddlers should note that there is no easy way out of the river before Avon.

Description After the first exciting drop, the Genesee becomes a big slow river meandering through a flood plain about 2 mi wide. The steep banks, at first wooded, soon become muddy and eroded. At lower water levels large sand bars are revealed. The gradient is so low that even small tributaries have threaded more than one mouth. Only at flood stage does the river have a strong current; then it can be very powerful, with strong eddies at the bends, many channels at the oxbows, and plenty of debris. The high steep banks, however, often give the paddler the sensation of being in a narrower river.

In the first exciting 1.5 mi below the dam, the river flows E and drops about 30 ft in Class I to II rapids. In spite of the gradient, there are some meanders in the last part of this stretch. Then the Genesee turns sharply N as Canaseraga Creek enters from the south. About 1 mi farther, in a long straight stretch with good current, the remains of the long-abandoned Jones Rd bridge are passed at a cable crossing. One mile farther power lines, a large manufacturing plant to the east, and a pronounced U-turn in the river indicate that the canoeist is about to arrive at the Rt 20A/Rt 39 bridge.

This is the earliest possible launch for those who wish to avoid the rough fast water just below Mt. Morris, or a possible takeout for those who do not enjoy the flat water to come. Access with parking is E of the bridge on the south side. If the bank near the bridge is too muddy, access is possible over riprap on the other side of the U, only about 50 yds S of the road a short distance farther E of the bridge.

About 2 mi farther Beards Creek comes in L and Little Beard Creek enters on the same side after another 2 mi. On the hill E is the campus of SUNY Geneseo. Below it near the river is the small National Warplane Museum. Since it takes the river almost 6 mi to cover a 2-mi airline distance between the two Geneseo bridges, the paddler has plenty of opportunity to see the view from all angles.

The second Geneseo bridge carries Rt 63 across the river and is not a good access point, nor are there any better ones in the next 20 mi. The 2 mi approaching the Fowlerville bridge and the 5 mi below it are pleasant canoeing. The stream is narrower, the banks are wooded and steep, and there is a sense of isolation. About .5 mi before the end of the trip at Avon, Conesus Creek enters R.

Takeout The canoeist will see a green metal bridge ahead and select a landing L upstream or downstream depending on water level. This should be scouted when cars are placed here. Parking is just E of the bridge on the north side, necessitating a carry across the bridge; landing immediately below the parking lot is not feasible. This bridge carries US 20 and Rt 5 across the Genesee just W of Avon, N.Y., and is 3.5 mi W of the intersection of these routes with I-390.

Genesee River

Counties: Livingston, Monroe

Segment ↕ Avon to Rochester (Ford St bridge)

Length ↔ 26 mi (Sections can be done as round trips from Rochester at less than HH levels)

Drop ↘ 9 ft

Difficulty ① Class I

Problems None (powerful river at flood stage)

Maps Caledonia, Rush, W. Henrietta, Rochester W, Rochester E; DeLorme pp 57, 71, 72

Contributor Daan Zwick

Launch Upstream access point for this trip is at Rts 5 & 20 bridge W of Avon. (See previous entry.)

Description The Genesee is now a large, slow-moving river, powerful in time of flood. It flows at first between steep, brushy banks, with houses high above the river E and a narrow strip of woods W. It soon slows down in a series of convolutions that make the paddler expect to meet himself coming back. There are oxbow lakes, the remains of old channels, some still connected to the river, others now separate. At H level, several of these can be explored, including Horseshoe and Log ponds. About 7 mi from launch the route passes the mouth of Honeoye Creek, which is canoeable. The usual takeout for the Honeoye Creek run is a RR bridge .25 mi upstream from the mouth. (See p 126.) This makes a good intermediate access point for those who find 26 mi a long day trip; a better one is at the Rt 253 bridge described below.

At about the 10-mi point a water tower, which marks the state correctional facility for youths at Industry, N.Y., can be seen on a hill R. Just N of this, the Rt 251 bridge is *not* a good access point. Oatka Creek, a delightful run at H levels, enters L 1.5 miles farther. (See p. 127.) The Rt 253 bridge, .5 mi farther, offers excellent access L at a state-maintained site. It is reached via Rt 253 from Scottsville or, on the other side, from the ever-present E. River Rd.

One mile downstream is the I-90 bridge, after which signs of beaver activity can be seen on both banks as the route passes the Kodak Training Center and Rochester Institute of Technology, both R. It is not known whether the human engineers learn from the beaver or vice versa. More houses appear and roads are closer as the route enters metropolitan Rochester. Ballantyne Bridge (Rt 252) is 6 mi beyond the Thruway; a few hundred yards farther Black Creek enters L. There is an excellent access point a few hundred yards upstream on this creek. (See p 138.) Three miles N of Black Creek, the Genesee intersects the New York State Barge Canal. The level of the river and canal here is maintained at 512 ft above sea level by a dam on the river 3.5 mi downstream, near the center of Rochester. It is possible to paddle past Genesee Valley Park (the recommended takeout) under the Elmwood Ave bridge, past the University of Rochester, and on toward the dam in order to obtain a fine view of downtown Rochester, but when the current is strong it is best to turn back upstream when Ford St, the last bridge before the dam, is reached.

Takeout A good access point is on Red Creek under I-390 in Genesee Valley Park. This is at the SE "corner" of the intersection of the Barge Canal and the Genesee. There is good parking. It is reached from Elmwood Ave in Rochester by entering the park at the signal light just S of the University of

Rochester campus and following the road through the park and over the canal. The next right turn leads to the Red Creek access. Another good access point, particularly for starting upstream on a round trip, is the public livery in the park. (At this writing, the City of Rochester is constructing additional boating access points in this general area.)

Genesee River

County: Monroe

Segment ↕ Mouth (Lake Ontario) to Rochester Lower Falls and return

Length ↔ 12 mi (round trip)

Drop ↘ 5 ft

Difficulty ① Class I

Problems ✲ None

Maps Rochester W, Rochester E; DeLorme pp 71, 72

Contributor Daan Zwick

Launch There are excellent public launching facilities with parking on the west bank near the mouth of the river. They can be reached by a well marked access road running E from Lake Ave, about .25 mi N of the Lake Ontario Parkway in Rochester.

Description This stretch from the jettied channel running out into Lake Ontario to the last of the many large waterfalls on the Genesee River is in the heart of Rochester, but it affords a surprising sense of wilderness. The lowest mile is lined with marinas, and power boats speed noisily up and down in season, but much of the upper 3 mi passes through a high wooded gorge. There are three parks in that stretch, Maplewood and Turning Point on the west bank and Seneca on the east. Turning Point Park is another good access point, especially for exploring upstream, but a locked gate here may require a 200-yd carry. Colonies of beaver live and work here, red-tailed hawks nest in the gorge, and great blue herons and several varieties of ducks fly up at the paddler's approach, only to light around the next bend.

On the hill just SW of the launch point is the Charlotte Lighthouse, built in 1822 and now a museum. From launch, the route passes under a RR swing bridge, usually open, and then a lift bridge. After about 1 mi the vistas become more natural, with cattails, an old beaver lodge, and wooded banks on both sides. At mi 2, the steep red wall of Rattlesnake Point is passed L and the turning basin is reached. This was a busy water terminus in the early 20th century; now only cement boats from Canada unload here.

The next 2 mi are in the deep gorge, with only parks and cemeteries at the top of the high banks. The Kodak wastewater treatment plant is passed R; the route goes first under a high arch carrying sewer pipes and a pedestrian footbridge, then under the even higher arch of Veterans Memorial Bridge. From this point on current can be felt; in season the banks may be lined with fishermen trying for salmon. The west bank is still parkland; on the east are a highrise apartment building, Rochester School for the Deaf, and Eastman Kodak. Driving Park Ave bridge is about the upstream limit for all but the strongest and most skillful paddlers, who may be able to reach the more quiet pool at the base of Lower Falls. The falls should not be approached. There is a short run through Class I rapids, accounting for almost all of the 5-ft drop on this trip, back to the fast and boulder-strewn water under Driving Park Ave, but most paddlers will be content to turn around at the bridge.

Takeout The trip can be ended at any of the access points mentioned above.

Black Creek (Allegany County)

County: Allegany

Segment Tibbetts Hill Rd to mouth (Genesee River)

Length 12 mi

Drop 190 ft (a 32 ft drop is bypassed)

Difficulty Class II

Problems Rapids, "interesting" carries

Maps Black Creek, Angelica; DeLorme p 42

Contributor Daan Zwick

Launch Access is possible where Tibbetts Hill Rd crosses the creek less than a mile E of the village of Black Creek, which is on Rt 305 about 5 mi NE of Cuba. Launch can be either upstream or down from the bridge; parking is possible on the shoulder of this local road.

Description New York is full of Black Creeks; this is one of three tributaries of the Genesee by that name. It is a small, shallow stream characterized by sharp turns, narrow channels, and fast current. Most of this run is Class I water, with many sections that are Class II. The creek can only be run at H levels.

The surroundings during the first 5 mi, from launch to the Rt 305 bridge, are partly farmland and partly wooded, and the next mile to Rockville Lake is totally wooded. Part of this stretch is in the bed of the abandoned Genesee Valley Canal, and this allows for a very unusual short round trip, as follows: Leave the creek by a short slackwater channel R just before the lake is reached. This channel ends at a 15-ft high earth dam. Relaunch in the lake after climbing the dam and paddle R along the dam. Then turn R again from the lake into a channel which is part of the former canal. After about 1 mi, traveling W, the paddler comes to the stream down below, flowing E. He can land, carry a few feet down to the previously run creek, and enjoy another downstream run to the lake. After making this loop as many times as desired, the canoeist can paddle E across the lake instead of following the bank to the R, land near the road on the other side of the lake, and carry over the hill to the L and down to a relaunch into the creek at Lake Rd bridge.

Caution ✖ The short stretch of Black Creek that passes by the lake should be avoided by using the above route. This section is in a narrow, boulder-strewn gorge.

The 4 mi remaining to the Genesee River are fast and rocky, dropping about 30 ft per mi, partly in a narrow gorge. This is definitely Class II water almost all the way. Depending on water level, some portions may require stopping and scouting.

Takeout Rt 19 crosses Black Creek a few yards above the mouth and provides access. Takeout is downstream from the bridge, L or R depending on water level. Cars should be parked on the shoulder of the road well away from the bridge.

Honeoye Creek

Counties: Ontario, Livingston, Monroe

Segment Pierpont Rd to mouth (Genesee River)

Length 25 mi (4 mi skipped at Honeoye Falls)

Drop 215 ft(110 skipped in car portage; 20 skipped in carry around Rush dam)

Difficulty Above N. Bloomfield, Class I (Class II at HH level); below Sibleyville, Class I; below Rush, Class I

Problems Portages, fallen trees, ability to maneuver quickly in fast water required.

Maps Honeoye, Honeoye Falls, Rush; DeLorme pp 58, 57

Contributor Daan Zwick

Launch Three miles N of the village of Honeoye, where Cty Rt 15 (Pierpont Rd) crosses Honeoye Creek, is a state-designated parking and stream access area. It is reached by taking US 20 13 mi W from Canandaigua, then turning S on Cy Rt 37 5.5 mi to its intersection with 15. The bridge is about .1 mi E of this spot. If the parking area is crowded, there is plenty of room for cars at the southeast corner of the intersection.

Description Honeoye (Honey-oy) Creek is a small seasonal stream, generally flowing through wooded valleys and remote from houses, especially above US 20. It gets very little use, either by paddlers or fishermen, and has a wilderness atmosphere. Like some other trips in this guide, this one is not very difficult if a car portage is made around the falls. The falls are totally unrunnable, and the stretch just above them is very difficult. The first section described is not runnable at L water levels.

One mile from launch the route passes under Rt 37. This is the only bridge in the fast and tricky 8.5 mi stretch down to the recommended takeout at the US 20 bridge near W. Bloomfield. Since this small stream passes through thick woods, there can be fallen trees or hanging branches lurking around each bend. About halfway through this stretch comes a series of remarkable loops, as the creek seems to be trying to bite its own tail. The average gradient here is about 12 ft per mi. The bridges and roads in this stretch shown on maps are either no longer extant or are private lanes.

Takeout is recommended on river R at US 20 about a mile W of W. Bloomfield, just upstream of the bridge. The access is from Pond Rd, which goes S from 20 just E of the bridge. (It is called Factory Hollow Rd on USGS Honeoye Falls Quad.) There is limited parking at the access point, but cars can be moved out to the shoulder of 20 after loading boats for a carry by car 3 mi W to Lima, then 4.25 mi N to Sibleyville on Rt 15A and .25 mi E on Sibley Rd to the launch point at the bridge. Parking is feasible on the shoulder of Sibley Rd away from the bridge.

Note ☞ It is possible to continue to N. Bloomfield and take out above the large ledges, but there is no public access there. Landowners, if asked, may or may not grant permission. It is also possible for experts in covered boats to run the ledges at H water level as far as the village of Honeoye Falls. It is NOT possible to run the falls. If the ledges are run, takeout should be scouted in advance at one of the several road bridges upstream of the village. It is definitely not safe to go all the way to the falls to take out.

After launch at Sibleyville on the right bank upstream of the bridge, the route continues about 4 mi with good current between wooded banks, first N to the abandoned Rochester Junction RR complex, then generally W until the slack water caused by the dam at Rush is reached. There is about a mile of slack water, extending to the dam in the center of Rush, just E of the Rt 15A bridge. Takeout is L (S) above the dam; there is a small park and parking area. The canoe livery here is open only in summer. To relaunch below the dam, paddlers carry their canoes across the bridge, using the east sidewalk, and put in below the dam but above the bridge. While there is no parking here, stream access is much easier on this side. The run below the dam, about 6 mi to the Genesee River, has no difficulties at MH level except for possible log jams, which vary from year to year. In 1991, there was a substantial one at the 1-mi point near the first RR bridge, which necessitated a haulover. A smaller down tree about 1 mi before takeout was negotiated R at H water level; at lower levels it might require a short carry. About 3 mi below the dam, the creek goes under I-390; there is a public access site here on the right bank directly under the high bridge. While it is possible to canoe into the Genesee, there is no convenient access from there.

Takeout A practical access point is L upstream of the RR bridge about .25 mi above the confluence. Parking is nearby at the top of the bank where Golah Rd ends at the RR tracks. Golah Rd goes W from E. River Rd about .5 mi S of the hamlet of W. Rush.

Oatka Creek

County: Wyoming

Segment ↕ Warsaw to Pearl Creek

Length ↔ 22 mi

Drop ↘ 35 ft

Difficulty ① Class I

Problems ✻ Possible log jams; at flood stage, may not be possible to go under some bridges

Maps Dale, Wyoming; DeLorme pp 56, 57

Contributor ✍ Daan Zwick

Launch Rt 19 follows the valley of Oatka Creek (Wyoming Valley) from Warsaw to LeRoy and provides easy access to the stream at several points. The first recommended launch point is at the Buffalo Rd bridge just northwest of Warsaw. This is reached by taking I-90 to its interchange with I-490 and Rt 19 (LeRoy exit), then going S on Rt 19, 20.6 mi, to turn W on Buffalo Rd. A sign marks the turn, which is just N of a McDonald's restaurant. There is adequate parking here.

Description ✏ Rising in the hills of Wyoming County near the town of Oatka, Oatka Creek is a tributary of the Genesee River. It flows N approximately to Buttermilk Falls, then turns sharply E to reach the Genesee near Scottsville. Above LeRoy, it drains a wide agricultural valley as a slow-moving stream. Below LeRoy it is a fast-moving trout stream with steeper wooded banks and some white water at H levels. For all practical purposes, it is not canoeable above Warsaw.

The stretch described here can be done at MH or higher levels in the spring or after a rain with few interruptions, although there may be a few short portages around debris dams or fallen trees. It is more exciting paddling at flood stage, but the canoeist should be prepared to stop and carry around a couple of abandoned bridges S of Wyoming. There may be insufficient clearance under them.

Warsaw to Wyoming: The stream meanders through a wide, steep-sided valley, with the steeper slope to the W. Because of the extensive meanders, mileages given are only approximate. Landmarks keep reappearing in different directions and tailwinds become headwinds. There are few bridges; Rt 19 crosses about 2.5 miles from launch. Some of the pastures are long abandoned, and signs of man and his handiwork are few. Banks are apt to be soft and muddy; at HH level stream-side trees provide the only sign of the creek's edges. After about 14 mi, Wyoming is reached.

It is possible to break the trip here, taking out where School Rd dead-ends L at an abandoned bridge. This access point, which may be the first possible launch at M water, is reached by car by driving S from Wyoming .5 mi to the southern boundary of the village and turning E by Wyoming High School. On the USGS Wyoming Quad, School Rd is called Mill Rd and shown as a through route, but this is no longer accurate. Parking is not difficult along this little-used road. According to Wyoming officials the building will no longer be used as a school after 1991.

Wyoming to Pearl Creek: This 8-mi stretch is similar to that described above. After School Rd two bridges in rapid succession and the Wyoming sewage treatment plant, R, are passed. The Wyoming Valley gradually widens out, and Oatka Creek wanders a few miles through a swamp before the Rt 19 bridge at the village of Pearl Creek is reached. At

H levels the approach to the bridge becomes a pond, but at lower levels there is only a small channel.

Takeout Rt 19 crosses the stream W of Pearl Creek; access is on the downstream side of the east bank. Parking is possible on the shoulder off the bridge.

Oatka Creek

Counties: Wyoming, Genesee

Segment Pearl Creek to LeRoy

Length 13 mi

Drop 45 ft

Difficulty Class I, higher at flood stage

Problems None

Maps Wyoming, Stafford, LeRoy; DeLorme pp 56, 57

Contributor Daan Zwick

Launch Access is at Rt 19 bridge, Pearl Creek. (See previous entry.) At L water levels, this may be the highest possible launch point.

Description Just below this launch, Oatka Creek is augmented by Pearl Creek entering R and one of New York's myriad Black Creeks L, and both volume and speed are increased. The surroundings become more wooded and the water a bit clearer as the current picks up. About 2 mi from launch a minor bridge is reached, and immediately thereafter the paddler is in Genesee County, although no significant change in surroundings is evident.

At about the 4-mi mark, an intermediate takeout point is reached at River Rd in Pavilion. It is on the west bank just before the Rt 63 bridge. This is reached by driving W on 63 from Pavilion and turning S on River Rd immediately after crossing the bridge. The access point is between the road and the creek, just S of Rt 63. Adequate parking is available on River Rd.

About 6.5 mi from launch, Oatka Creek passes under Rt 20. Now the gradient has increased from a negligible foot or two per mile to a noticeable 5 ft per mile. The stream becomes faster and clearer and, after the turn to the northeast near the E. Bethany Rd, riffles begin to appear, only to disappear as the dam impoundment is reached. The northeast turn also marks the entrance of White Creek L, but its mouth is lost in a marshy area.

As the route enters the slack water above the dam, the paddler sees an abandoned RR bridge and other signs of a town.

Takeout Just R of the dam, near the power station, access is possible. By road, this point is reached by turning W from Rt 19 on the first road S of the Oatka Creek bridge. This is .5 mi S of the main intersection with Rt 5 in the center of LeRoy.

Caution At HH or higher stages, it is wiser to take out just upstream of the bridge at Cole Rd, which is reached via the E. Bethany Rd. Cole Rd is a left turn 2 mi SE of the Rt 5 and E. Bethany Rd intersection in LeRoy. Signs mark these roads.

Note While it is possible to carry to and paddle the dammed-up pond in the center of LeRoy, the rest of the 4-mi stretch to Buttermilk Falls is not canoeable. To continue canoeing Oatka Creek, a motor portage to the Oatka Trail is recommended. (See next entry.)

Oatka Creek

Counties: Genesee, Monroe

Segment ↕ Buttermilk Falls to Scottsville

Length ↔ 17 mi

Drop ↘ 135 ft

Difficulty ① Class I

Problems ✻ Dam at Wheatland Center, possible log jams

Maps Churchville, Caledonia, Clifton, West Henrietta; DeLorme p 71

Contributor ✍ Daan Zwick

Launch Oatka Trail, which in spite of its name is a road, is reached by taking Rt 19 about 1 mi S from I-90 (LeRoy Exit) to Oatka Trail at the bottom of Fort Hill. (A good view of Buttermilk Falls can be had by driving an additional .75 mi and walking E along the RR tracks a short distance.) About .5 mi from Rt 19, Oatka Trail is very close to the creek. This is the launch point. Parking is available nearby on the south side of the road.

Description ✏ This is a fun run at MH to H water levels. It is not usually runnable in midsummer except after a rain. The banks are generally wooded with a few farms interspersed. Skill is required to maneuver longer canoes around some sharp bends. The water is clear and cold, which accounts for the presence of several small drops over weirs made to improve the trout fishing. Although the weirs extend from bank to bank, it is usually possible to run them in the center, where there is a smooth lip. The amount of drop ranges from 12 to 20 in. Near these weirs fishing clubs jealously guard their posted banks.

Oatka Creek • Weir on Oatka Creek

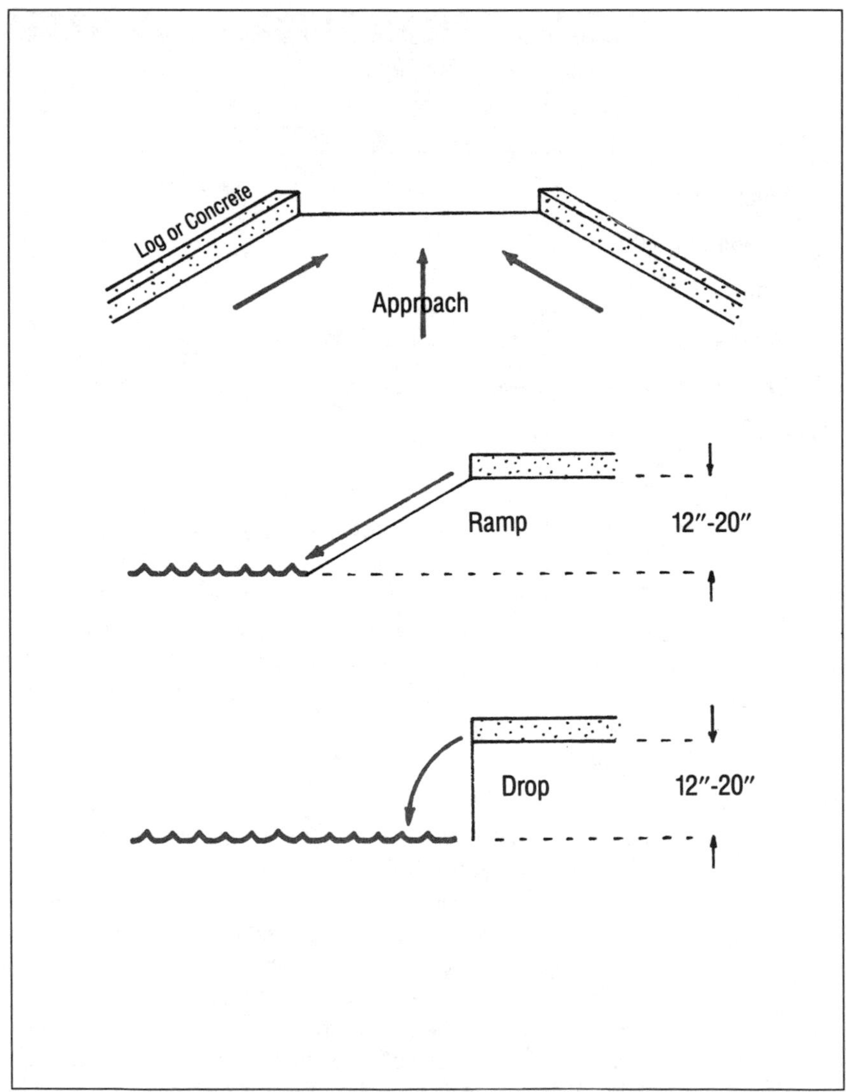

In the launch area the south bank is white with a profusion of trillium in spring, and about .25 mi upstream a rare variety with a green center is found. A steep, hundred-foot cliff is to the right; occasional similar cliffs are L during the first few miles. About .5 mi from launch, the Perry Rd bridge is reached. About 4 mi farther, the creek bends sharply S and Mad Creek enters R. At the 6-mi point, the stream passes under the Rt 36 bridge, just N of Mumford. This is a possible intermediate takeout point; parking is possible at a nearby gas station if permission is asked in advance.

The dam at Wheatland Center 3 mi farther impounds, for almost a mile above it, the only slack water on the trip. The dam requires a short carry L which at some water levels is difficult but not dangerous. Paddlers should move L well above the dam to avoid being pulled with current into a dangerous sluiceway. The dam is reached by car by taking Rt 383 W for 3.5 mi from Scottsville, then turning S on the Wheatland Center Rd.

About 2 mi below the dam near the Union St bridge at Garbutt, the remains of a small wooden dam (surmounted by metal spikes!) should be scouted before running. At H water level, it can be run in the center; lower water may require negotiating the far right end or lining the canoe down over the dam. At this writing, there is a large log jam about 2 mi farther. This can be avoided at H water by seeking out a channel L, but at lower water it requires a short carry. From the log jam it is only a short distance to the takeout point.

Takeout It is possible, with some dragging around fallen trees and gravel bars, to continue 1 mi to the Genesee and then to paddle .5 mi downstream to a state-maintained access R at Rt 253. Most canoeists prefer to end the trip at the Scottsville town park just E of the village at the Rt 251 bridge, downstream R. There is plenty of parking as well as picnic facilities.

Black Creek (Monroe County)

Counties: Genesee, Monroe

Segment ↕ Churchville Dam to W. Sweden Rd and return

Length ↔ 16 mi round trip

Drop ↘ 5 ft

Difficulty ① Class I

Problems ✲ None

Maps Churchville; DeLorme p 71

Contributor Daan Zwick

Launch A convenient public launch site with sufficient parking is at the west end of the dam in Churchville. It is reached by turning N at the west end of the Rt 33 bridge, about 200 yds E of the traffic light at the intersection of Rts 36 and 33. Churchville is 1 mi N of the Rt 36 exit from I-490.

Description This Black Creek, one of three tributaries of the Genesee by that name, rises very near the Genesee/Wyoming county line E of Attica but is not usually canoed above W. Sweden Rd for the reason given below. The stretch described is ideal for beginning paddlers and is canoeable except when actually frozen over. There are no difficulties anywhere on the route except the abandoned road described below, and the first 4 mi above the dam are slack water. Very few motorboats are in evidence, and most of these are low-powered fishing boats. Many ducks, geese, and other waterfowl, as well as shore birds, frequent the area.

The route goes generally N for the first .5 mi, with houses visible on the shore. When the water is warm part of this section is clogged with aquatic plants, but the clear channel is easy to follow. The route turns W and enters Churchville Park, a Monroe County park. The channel moves from one side of the slack water to the other. In dry seasons it is possible to stray from the channel and run aground.

The park boundary on the south bank, marked by the appearance of cottages, is reached first. At this point the channel becomes more definite and the stream begins to wind, with woods S and a golf course N. The golf course is soon left behind; now both banks are uninhabited and wooded, and current begins to make itself felt. The Rt 19 bridge is about 3 mi from launch. It is possible to land here, but there is no legal parking in the vicinity.

A few hundred yards farther upstream the route enters a large swamp, most of which is included in the Bergen (Ber-jen) Swamp Wildlife Sanctuary. At this point is an abandoned farm road, under which the stream flows in two culverts. Depending upon water level, it is possible to (1) push the canoe through a culvert; (2) haul the canoe over the obstacle; or (3) paddle right over the road. Beyond here at L water the channel is about 10 ft wide, and at H water it is lost in the flooded forest. Near here on the left bank is a fish and game club; permission can sometimes be obtained to park and launch or take out here. Inquiry should be made at the large stone house on Rt 19 just S of the bridge.

The W. Sweden Rd 8 mi from the dam is the usual turnaround for this trip. In very dry weather, paddlers may have to turn back at the culverts; at very high water levels, beginners may also be turned back here by the strength of the current, but neither is usually the case. The return trip is usually quicker than the first half, not so much because of current as because of the prevailing westerlies. For most of the trip, the effect of current is secondary to that of wind.

Takeout Normally there is no hazard in the return approach to the launch at the dam, since the channel at this point is near the west bank. With a strong north wind, paddlers should hug the right bank when approaching the takeout.

Note Permission is necessary to canoe W of W. Sweden Rd. It may be obtained in person, by mail, or by telephone from Patti Kowski, Custodian, Bergen Swamp Society, 6646 Hessenthaler Rd., Byron, NY 14422; tel. (716) 548-7304.

Black Creek (Monroe County)

County: Monroe

Segment Churchville Dam to mouth (Genesee River)

Length About16 mi (very meandering)

Drop 35 ft

Difficulty Class I

Problems Remains of dam, down trees, abandoned RR bridge

Maps Churchville, Clifton, W. Henrietta; DeLorme p 71

Contributor Daan Zwick

Launch The access point is on river R about 200 yds below Churchville Dam. It is reached from the rear of the shopping plaza on the east side of Rt 36 about 200 yds S of the traffic signal in Churchville. Cars may be parked at the back of the plaza and boats carried down the bank to the creek.

Description The first 8 mi of this segment of Black Creek, to Union St, can only be run at MH or better level. The lowest 3 mi, from Rt 252 to the Genesee River, can be navigated any time the ice is out; from the recommended takeout this makes a good round trip for beginners, the only problems being finding the correct channel and negotiating down trees.

The first 200 yds after launch has the highest gradient of this trip; at lower than MH level some lining down may be necessary. At the 1-mi point, the creek passes under I-490 and turns E. Sometimes the banks are wooded, sometimes back yards are seen, and occasionally farmland comes right to the edge of the stream. Two bridges are passed, the first being Burnt Mill Rd and the second Attridge Rd, about 4 mi from launch. About 2.5 mi farther the creek goes under Rt 33A. Just beyond this is a broken-down narrow dam. This should be examined before running; unfortunately, the local landowner has been known to object to canoeists landing to scout this obstacle. It is basically a short, rocky pitch with a quiet pool below, in which a sharp left turn must be made.

Beyond this point Black Creek Park borders the stream for a short distance R. A few hundred yards farther, the Rt 259 (Union St) bridge marks the halfway point of the trip. The next 8 mi is mostly in a swamp, with a meandering stream bed occasionally blocked by fallen trees. This is particularly true for the final 3 mi below Rt 252. This stretch would seem very remote from civilization if it were not directly in the flight path of Rochester Monroe County Airport. The stream winds and sometimes divides around islands, particularly at H water levels. The large stone bridge of an abandoned RR is about .5 mi before takeout. At highest water levels, boats may not be able to pass under the arches of this bridge and must be carried L, but this is an unusual condition.

Caution Do not enter the arch unless certain that there is enough clearance. Beyond this bridge the stream takes a fairly direct course E to its mouth.

Takeout Canoeists should land L upstream of the Rt 383 (Scottsville Rd) bridge, which is just above the mouth. This spot is about 3.5 mi S of the Scottsville Rd exit of I-390 and is reached by turning W at the Castle Inn parking lot and driving to the south end of the packed dirt field. There is sufficient parking close to the creek.

• • • • LAKE ONTARIO DRAINAGE—WEST

Alice Broberg

Owasco Outlet, upstream from Throopsville access bridge (p. 205, Barge Canal–Finger Lakes watershed).

Lake Ontario Drainage, Eastern Part
Part V

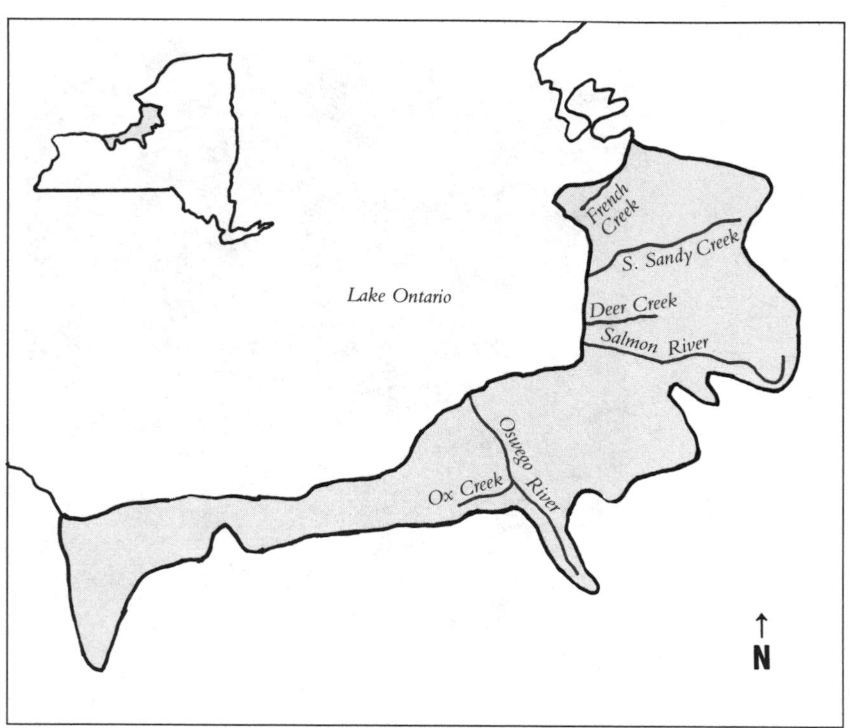

Oswego River

Counties: Oswego, Onondaga

Segment ↕ Phoenix to Fulton

Length ↔ 9 mi, without side trips

Drop ↘ Negligible

Difficulty ① Class I

Problems ✻ Possible strong current at launch and takeout; see text

Maps Baldwinsville, Pennellville, Fulton; DeLorme p 74

Contributor ✍ Daniel Geist

Launch There are a number of possible points of access to the river between Phoenix and Fulton. The first is at Phoenix, at the Culvert St lift bridge, on the island below the dam and lock. It is a rocky launch point.

Note ☞ It is possible to launch at Henley Park (see p 202), but this necessitates locking through, which is only possible when the canal is open (May 1 to November). Lock operators must be notified in advance and may be reluctant to lock canoes through in the company of other boats. Anywhere in the vicinity of a dam or lock, there may be strong swirling currents when the control gates are open. It is also possible to launch or take out at Bear Springs Recreational Area, off Rt 57. Another popular spot with canoeists and fishermen is below the Miller Brewing Company, on state land, where a short dirt road leads W to the river. This access point may be seen from Rt 57. There is ample parking at this spot.

Description The Oswego River is canalized for its entire length, from the source at Three Rivers to the mouth, where it empties into Lake Ontario at Oswego. Locks and dams control the flow; gradient is negligible between locks. This trip is more pleasant in spring before the canal is open to navigation or in fall when powerboat traffic is light. The banks are generally high and wooded, with many well kept and spacious riverside homes.

A possible detour following the old river channel occurs R about 3 mi below Phoenix at Buoy 32, just before Hinmansville. Between the old river and the canal is Walter Island. This route, about 1 mi long, is quite pretty, with wood ducks and herons, and wildflowers and mulberry trees along the bank. It also enables the canoeist to escape canal traffic for a short period.

At Bear Springs Recreation Area, 4 mi from Phoenix, R, a section of the old Oswego Canal parallels the route. It is navigable for 2 mi with a few short carries. Its isolation and the remains of old locks make this an interesting side trip. About 1.5 mi from Bear Springs, Ox Creek enters L. (See p 145.) At the Miller Brewing Company, by Buoy 69, the route divides, with the main commercial channel E of Big Island. An interesting back channel, suitable only for very shallow draft boats, winds to the W of these islands.

Takeout In addition to access points mentioned above, takeout is feasible at the City of Fulton Boat Launch off Rt 48 at Green St. Unfortunately, parking here is limited.

Caution ✖ If the water level is H and the gates are open, strong currents will be encountered here.

Oswego River

County: Oswego

Segment ↕ Fulton to Minetto

Length ↔ 7 mi, without side trip

Drop ↘ Negligible

Difficulty ① Class I

Problems ✻ Strong currents around dams, locks, and powerhouses

Maps Fulton, Oswego E; DeLorme p 74

Contributor Daniel Geist

Launch Access is at the Fulton City Boat Launch. There are two city launch sites; this one is below both dams and locks, off Rt 57 at the north end of the city.

Description This trip is in many ways similar to the preceding entry, which see. Among the beautiful riverside homes are the Van Buren Mansions, where relatives of that US President lived in the19th century. These are about 3 mi downstream from Fulton. Immediately thereafter, one of New York State's numerous Black Creeks enters E. A short but interesting side trip may be made up this tributary. Both below Black Creek and above Battle Island, just downstream from it, several old canal structures are worth landing and looking over. Battle Island and Battle Island State Park are so named because the island was the scene of a battle in the French and Indian War. The French ambushed and defeated a British resupply expedition enroute to the forts at Oswego.

Oswego River • Lock 5 at Minetto

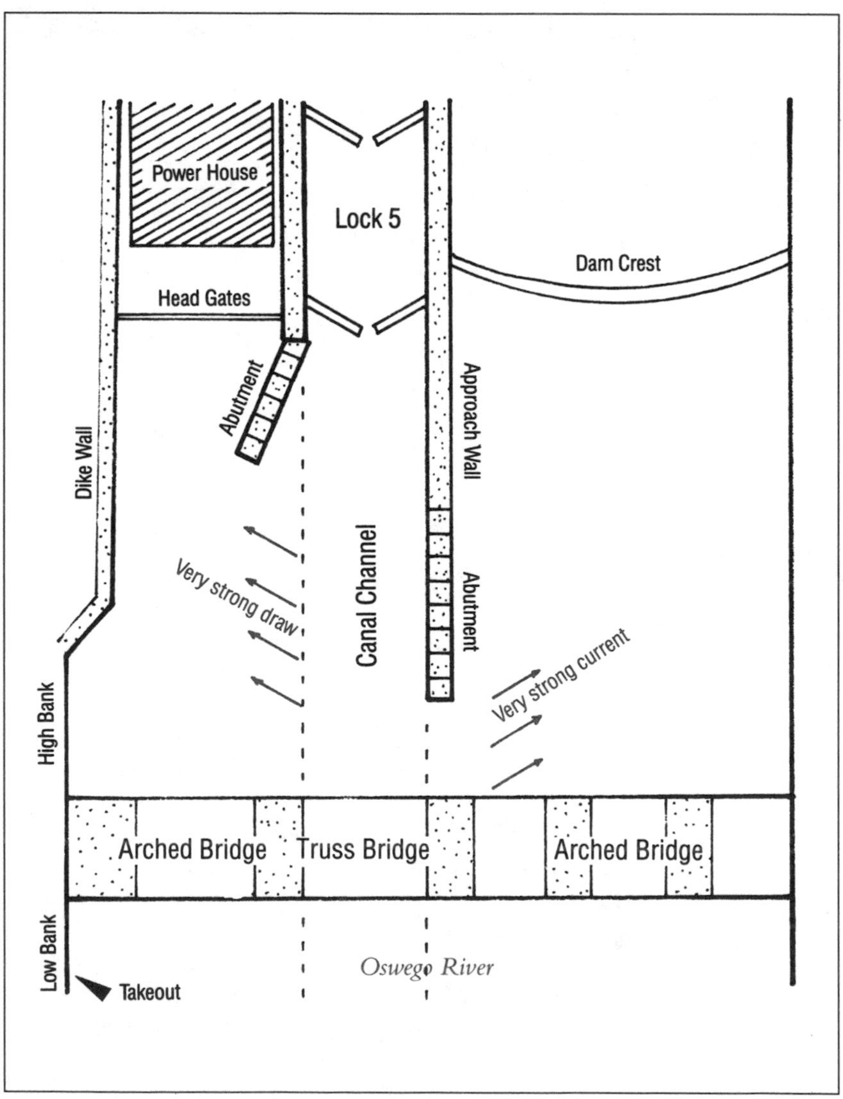

Below Battle Island, the old abandoned canal channel, E, makes an attractive side trip, involving a few short carries.

Takeout Recommended takeout is above Minetto Bridge, W, just off Rt 48. There is parking here for several cars; a village park is adjacent.

Note After consulting the lockkeeper, it is possible to lock through here and continue toward Oswego and Lake Ontario. However, this trip of slightly over 5 mi involves several additional locks.

Strong Caution Immediately downstream from Minetto Bridge, the dam and powerhouse associated with the lock create strong and confusing currents. Unless the canoeist has arranged to lock through, he should not travel past the recommended takeout point. Once past the bridge, there is no way to get off the river because the approach walls are very high and the draw from the powerhouse is very strong. This is probably the only place on the Oswego River where a canoeist can get into serious trouble. Even the seasoned skippers of powerful tugs have been known to use expletives in referring to this lock.

Ox Creek

County: Oswego

Segment Rt 55 (Jacksonville Rd) to mouth (Oswego River)

Length Round trip upstream, 10 mi; round trip downstream, 4 mi

Drop Negligible

Difficulty Class I

Problems ✻ Beaver dams, down trees (upper section)

Maps Fulton, Lysander; DeLorme p 74

Contributor Ron Schlie

Launch Note that easiest access is in the middle of the round trip, as it were. Travel S from Fulton on Rt 48 and turn W on Wybron Rd. Cross RR tracks; at T intersection turn N on County Rt 14 about .5 mi to bridge. There is plenty of parking room here.

Description ☞ Ox Creek is as much a marsh or river as a creek. In places, near the mouth, it is as wide as the Oswego it empties into. Upstream, the area will usually be flooded in early spring; there is a deep channel the rest of the year. Numerous geese and other waterfowl, spawning carp (in spring), deer and beaver may be seen on this trip.

The round trip begins by traveling upstream. The route enters cattails after about .75 mi; there is a low beaver dam in this area. When the stream appears to end, a current can be detected coming through the trees R. The canoeist can pick his way through the trees to the S. Granby Rd bridge, which is the limit of travel unless the marsh is in flood. Poling may be more effective than paddling at this point and beyond.

If the water is high, travel is possible above S. Granby Rd to the Jacksonville Rd bridge. The stream meanders, but the channel is generally to the R. There are down trees. In general, the water level determines how far the canoeist can go.

Returning to the launch point, the route now leads downstream. At about the .75 mi mark, the creek passes through a tunnel under the Conrail tracks. One mile farther, after

Ox Creek • Rt 55 (Jacksonville Rd) to mouth (Oswego River)

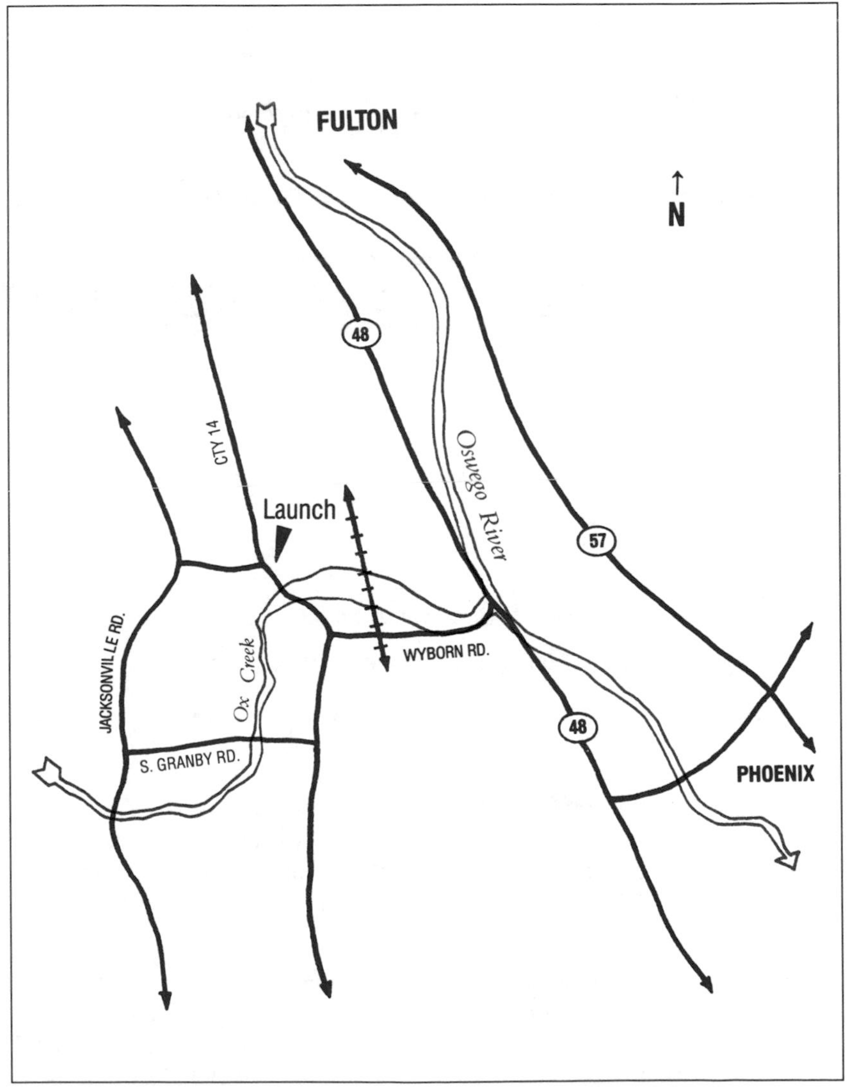

passing a number of camps and going under Rt 48, it emerges into the Oswego River. It is of course possible to paddle from this point L, downstream, to Fulton, Oswego, and Lake Ontario or R, upriver, to Phoenix and beyond, if desired.

Takeout For this round trip, takeout is at the launch point.

Salmon River Reservoir

County: Oswego

Segment Entire length

Length 12–14 mi, round trip

Drop Negligible

Difficulty Class I

Problems Large waves during windy periods

Maps Orwell, Redfield; DeLorme pp 83, 84

Contributor Ron Schlie

Launch Salmon River Reservoir is reached by traveling W from Pulaski on Cty Rt 2. There are two state boat launch areas on the north shore, just off this route. One, at the end of CCC Rd, is 1 mi from Rt 2; the other, at the end of Jackson Rd, is .5 mi.

Description There are several Salmon Rivers in New York, and that's not even counting Salmon Creeks. Like so many other good canoeing streams, this Salmon River rises on the Tug Hill Plateau and flows generally W to Lake Ontario. Dams for hydroelectric power have changed the nature of the river, but from the canoeist's point of view this is not all bad: The release of water makes the lower part canoeable in summer, while the reservoir described here is a delightful lake to canoe.

Salmon River Reservoir resembles Stillwater Reservoir in the Adirondacks: Except for a few camps on the north shore, much of it is quite remote and wild. The two access points described above are quite close together; launching at one and taking out at the other is not worthwhile, so any trip on this lake will be a round trip. The reservoir is 6 or 7 mi long; the round trip can take from a day to a month. The deep bay at the southwest end, in back of Hall Island, is interesting to explore and contains several active beaver colonies. The west tip of Hall Island is a good camping and picnic spot. Huckleberry and Burdick islands are also good for picnicking.

In the spring, when the water is high, the east end is a good place for exploration and viewing wildiife. Some areas E of Redfield are posted by a private club.

Caution ✖ As with any large lake, moderate to strong winds can produce, in a surprisingly short time, waves dangerous to canoeists.

Takeout At the end of the round trip, takeout is at whichever launch point was used.

Salmon River

County: Oswego

Segment ↕ Altmar to Lake Ontario

Length ↔ 13.5 mi

Drop ↘ 280 ft

Difficulty ③ Class III

Problems Strainers, rapids

Maps Richland, Pulaski; DeLorme p 83

Contributor Kevin Howells

Launch Access is just upstream of the only bridge in Altmar, on the south bank. Drive N on I-81 to Rt 13 exit just S of Pulaski. Take 13 E about 6 mi to a fork just W of Altmar. Go L at the fork on Pulaski Rd .7 mi to an intersection. The bridge is now immediately on the L. A small parking lot with a boat ramp is directly ahead; a larger parking lot is on the north side of Pulaski St just before the intersection. The best launch is at the boat ramp. Other possible access points are described on the next few pages.

Description The Salmon River is canoeable below the reservoir at most times because of the frequent water releases at the dam. The pulsing releases keep the river fairly free of ice in winter, and some extremely hardy souls do paddle it then. Information about releases can be obtained by calling (315) 298-6531; reports are updated each day at 5 PM. With a single generator release, water levels are adequate but scratchy; a two-generator release provides a good level. When water is coming over the dam, the river is for advanced paddlers only.

Pulaski is known as the "Salmon Capital of the East." In spring and fall, fishermen stand shoulder to shoulder along some stretches of the river. The section described here is definitely not for the beginner at any water level, but it provides an exciting and challenging ride that is deservedly popular with experienced whitewater enthusiasts. The trip is described in segments of about 3 mi each. It is obviously possible to do the entire 13.5 mi in one trip.

Altmar to Pineville, 3 mi: This section is mainly Class I rapids or less, but because of the strainers immediately below Altmar, paddlers should have the ability to maneuver in fast water and do eddy turns. Below the put-in the current quickly carries the paddler to the .5-mi point, where the river divides around several islands. The canoeist should keep to the main channels and watch for strainers. At the 1.5-mi point, there is a set of standing waves where the river passes some old RR bridge abutments, at which logs often collect. From here it is a pleasant paddle on fast water to the Pineville takeout on river R, 3 mi from launch. This access point is reached by car by turning N off Rt 13 at Pineville, crossing the bridge, and immediately turning R on Sheepskin Rd. Access, with a parking area, is between the road and the river just after this turn.

Pineville to Rt 2A bridge, 3.75 mi: This section is a good place for canoeists to acquire their first whitewater experience, under the guidance of more experienced paddlers. It begins with moving water and gradually builds to easy Class II rapids. There are several islands; paddlers should keep to the main channel and watch for strainers. At the 1.75-mi point is a Class I rapid; at 2 mi and 2.25 mi are Class II rapids. The easier course is usually R, the more challenging, L. The paddler should survey the situation and use his own judgment. Easy rapids continue from this point to the bridge, 3.75 mi from launch. The takeout is on the right bank, just before the bridge. This access point is reached by road by taking Rt 2A N from Rt 13 about 1 mi E of Pulaski. Immediately after crossing the river, turn R into the parking lot.

Rt 2A to Black Hole, 3.5 mi: This section begins with gentle rapids and builds to Class III water in Pulaski. It is a good place for intermediate paddlers to practice and develop their skills. After mild rapids for the first .5 mi, a Class II ledge is encountered. The easier route is L. Class I and II rapids continue past the RR bridge and around a bend L to the I-81 bridge at the 1.7-mi point. Down trees often collect around the abutments of this bridge. At 2 mi, the buildings of the Firemen's Field can be seen L. The river splits around a large island .25 mi farther. Those who wish to avoid more white water and some nasty strainers should take the right channel. To stay in the main current, cut left after the island. Below it a Class III rapids runs down to the Rt 11 bridge. Experts surf almost every wave and hole from here to the takeout. More Class II and III rapids lead to the S. Jefferson St bridge, 3 mi from launch, and Titanic Hole below it. Those who wish may take out at the Black Hole, .5 mi farther, on the R side. This is reached by car by taking Bridge St, Pulaski, to the sewage treatment plant, where there is ample parking. Paddlers must carry .1 mi to get beyond the plant fence. During peak fishing seasons a parking fee may be charged.

Black Hole to Port Ontario, 3 mi: Those continuing below the Black Hole will enjoy another .5 mi of Class II and III rapids, followed by mild rapids and riffles, and ending in the still waters of Port Ontario Bay. This bay makes a pleasant flatwater trip with lush green islands and many birds. In calm weather, the canoeist can enter Lake Ontario and paddle N 1 mi to Deer Creek. (See p 155.)

Takeout Those who take this trip in its entirety will take out on the left side of Port Ontario Bay before reaching the wooded dunes which separate the bay from the lake. This access point in Selkirk Shores State Park is reached via Pine Grove Rd,

Salmon River 1

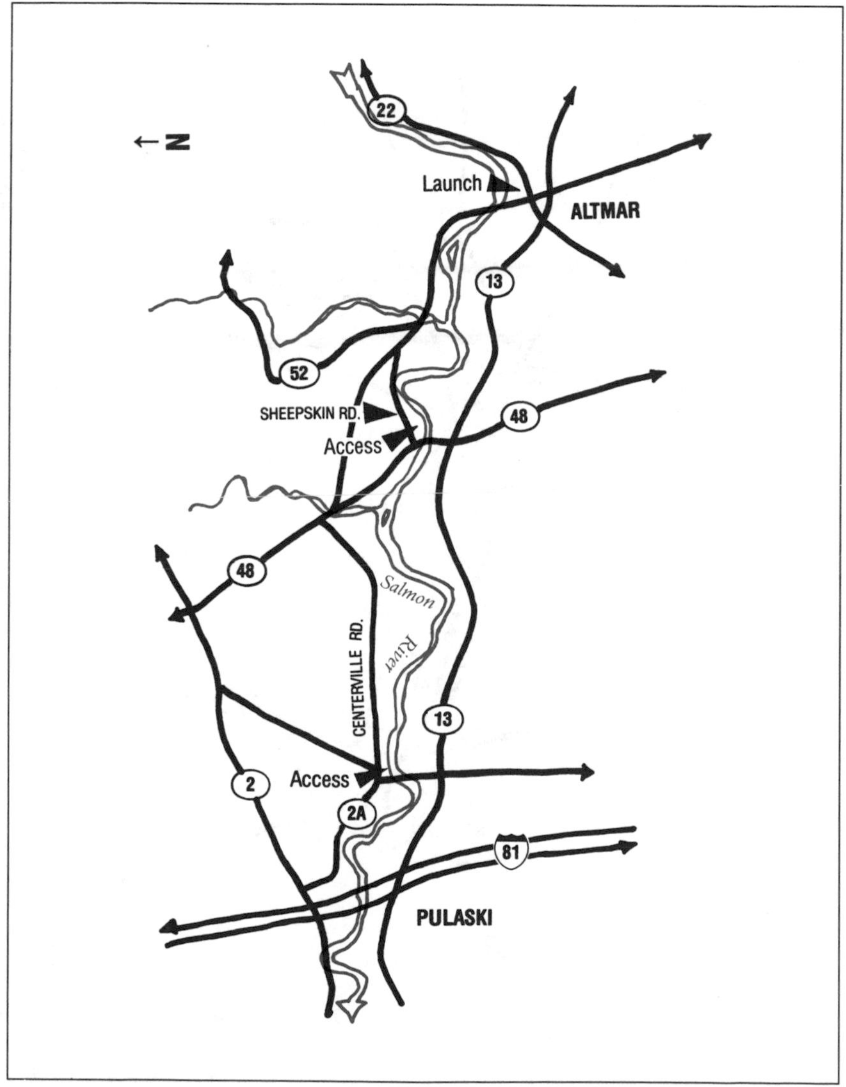

Salmon River 2

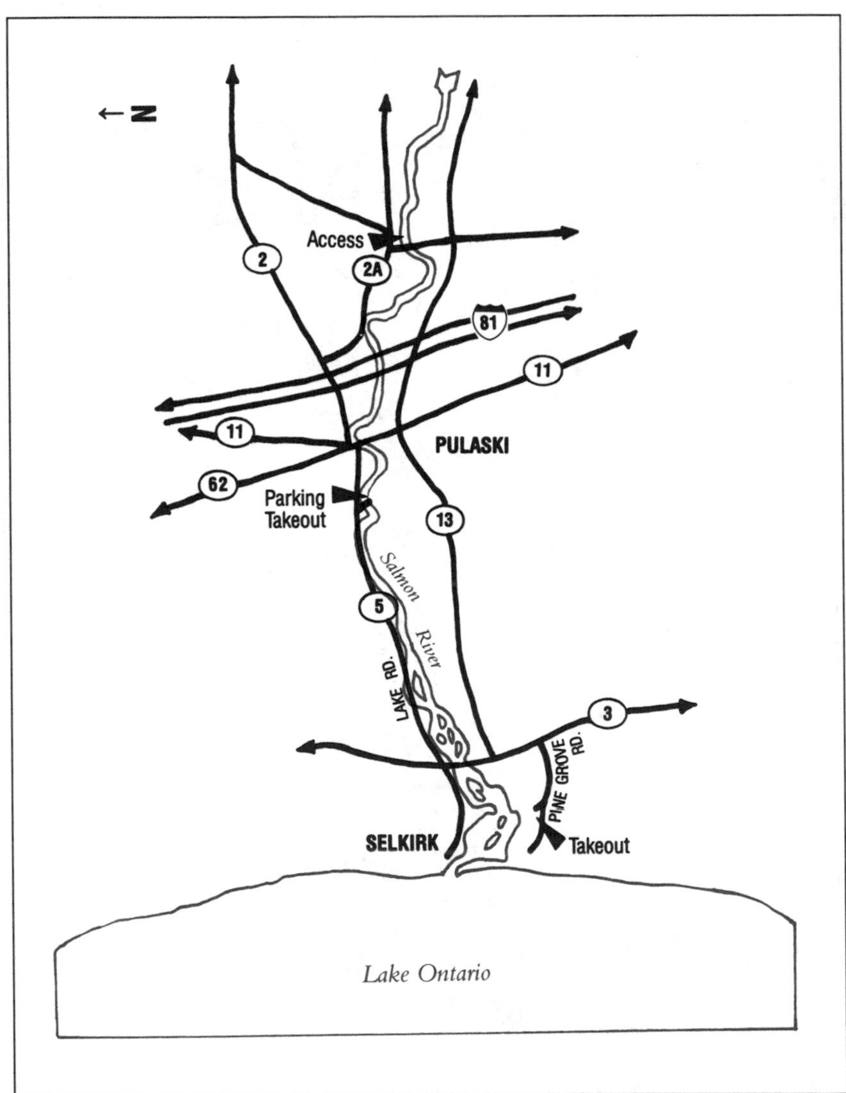

which is the first right turn off Rt 3, traveling S from Port Ontario. Camping, swimming, and the other usual activities are permitted in the park, and a day use fee is charged. There are also two state launch sites, catering to motorboats, on the north shore of the bay.

Deer Creek

County: Oswego

Segment ↕ Rt 3 to Lake Ontario

Length ↔ 4 mi

Drop ↘ Negligible

Difficulty ① Class I

Problems * Large waves on Lake Ontario, particularly during or after westerly winds

Maps Pulaski; DeLorme p 83

Contributor Ron Schlie

Launch There is a state boat launch site W of Rt 3, about 2.5 mi N of Port Ontario. On the stream, this point is just below the confluence of Deer and Little Deer creeks. Parking is readily available, but the canoe must be carried about 100 yds to the stream.

Description This area is in many ways similar to Lakeview, just N of here. (See p 159.) The creek winds through a marsh replete with wildlife: several varieties of duck, great blue herons, geese, terns, hawks, beaver, turtles, and many other creatures. Immediately after launch, a few small beaver dams may impede the waterway. Soon the route enters Deer Creek Marsh Wildlife Management Area, which, not surprisingly, teems with all kinds of wild life. Carp spawn here in the spring, and fishing is good, because large boats cannot obtain access to the area.

Continuing and heading W, the route enters the dune area. Here, about l mi from Lake Ontario, Deer Creek turns sharply S and parallels the dunes. Emerging into Lake Ontario, paddlers should be aware of the possibility of encountering dangerous waves. Picnicking is permitted here, but no fires and no overnight camping. Please take nothing but pictures and leave nothing but footprints. Canoeists who land should stay on the beach and avoid walking on the dunes, which comprise a very fragile ecosystem.

Takeout Retracing the route to the launch point, the canoeist exits the stream as he entered it. It is possible, depending on water level, to paddle upstream from the access point, but usually only about 100 yds.

South Sandy Creek (Lorraine Gulf)

County: Jefferson

Segment Bullock Corners to Rt 11

Length 11 mi

Drop 560 ft

Difficulty Class III, possibly approaching Class IV at higher water levels

Problems Small streams entering narrow deep shale gorge; numerous ledges, smooth shale chutes, possible strainers. Vertical walls 30 to 200 feet high abutting stream on outside corners. No gauges or public sources for levels, which vary greatly and rapidly.

Maps Adams, Rodman; DeLorme p 83

Contributors Kevin Howells and others

Launch To reach access point, take I-81 to Rt 178 (Adams) Exit. Stay on 178 E and S to Lorraine and 3.7 mi farther to Bullock Corners. Turn L here on unpaved road (Leepy Rd or Cty Rt 95), crossing South Sandy Creek on steel bridge after about .3 mi. Park on north side. There is a graded path down to the stream on the southwest side.

Description South Sandy Creek has cut a narrow winding gorge through the soft shale of the Tug Hill Plateau. Small tributary streams splash down the rock walls from the canyon rim. Cedar and hemlock sprout from cracks in the walls. The regular slope of the stream bed is broken occasionally by small ledges and pink granite boulders.

This trip can only be done at time of high water, after prolonged rains in spring or fall. There is no gauge. Look upstream from the takeout point, the Rt 11 bridge: If there is enough water to fill the riverbed well, the trip should be good. If it appears quite rocky, it would be best to go elsewhere. This stretch of S. Sandy Creek is similar to the Salmon River and the E Branch of Fish Creek. Rapids are continuous; at lower levels they are Class II and III. At higher levels, powerful wave trains and holes are the rule. Obviously, it should only be attempted by experienced

Lorraine Gulf • Bullock Corners to Rt 11

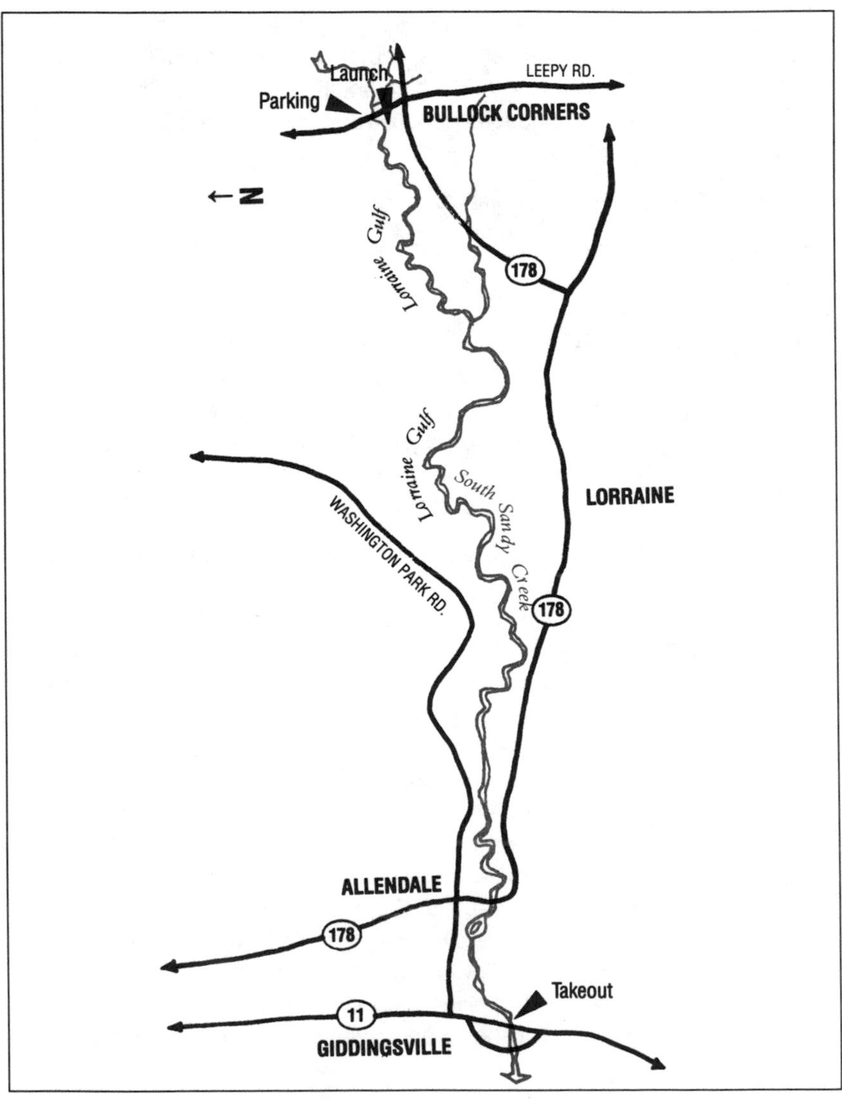

whitewater canoeists, in a group. Paddlers should have mastered the Eskimo roll.

Caution ✖ The gradient encountered in this trip, 50 ft per mi, is the highest of any listed in this guide.

At the launch point, S. Sandy Creek is quite small and winds through a narrow shady gorge. At 1.5 mi a stream plunges 20 ft from the right wall to join the creek spectacularly. At 2.3 mi a large hole lurks around a right-hand bend. The best route is to hug the right bank. The next mile is the steepest, dropping 70 ft. When Abijah Creek enters the gorge at 2.7 mi, the volume of the stream increases noticeably. Below this point the gorge widens, the walls are taller and sheerer, and the rapids are more powerful. Wave and hole rapids continue for the next 7 mi almost without interruption. As it passes under the Rt 178 bridge, 9.8 mi from the launch point, S. Sandy Creek emerges from the gorge. From this point the rapids moderate to Class II rock gardens, but frequent strainers still demand caution.

Takeout At the Rt 11 bridge, 2.5 mi S of Adams, takeout is possible on either side of the stream, although the north shore is probably easier. Parking for a limited number of cars is available on the highway shoulder.

South Sandy Creek (Lakeview Wildlife Management Area)

County: Jefferson

Segment ↕ Creek, marshes and ponds of the Wildlife Management Area

Length ↔ Various round trips may add up to as much as 12 mi; see text

Drop ↘ Negligible

Difficulty ① Class I

Problems ✻ Large waves on Lake Ontario under certain wind conditions

Maps Ellisburg; DeLorme p 83

Contributors ✍ Members of Ka-Na-Wa-Ke Canoe Club

Launch The general area is reached by traveling N on I-81 to the Rt 13 Exit just S of Pulaski, thence W on 13 to Rt 3 at Port Ontario and N on 3. There are three readily accessible launch sites. The most southerly of the three, the Montario Point launch site, is well marked. It is reached via a gravel road from Montario Point Rd, which intersects Rt 3 about a half mile N of the Jefferson County line. There is plenty of parking room.

Description ✏ The Lakeview Wildlife Management Area offers a number of safe and placid canoe routes. Many varieties of fish may be found in the ponds, streams, and channels, and the canoeist may glimpse kingfishers, great blue herons, kingbirds, marsh wrens, coots, and many other birds. One of the largest populations of black terns in the United States is found here. There is no legal camping, picnicking, or swimming, and the area is patrolled by game wardens. Southwick Beach State Park, immediately N of Lakeview, is a legal place to swim, picnic, and camp. The park charges the usual fees. Considerate canoeists and fishermen often carry out of Lakeview trash that they did not carry in.

From the first launch point, it is possible to canoe N through South Colwell Pond and continue through North Colwell Pond. ("Colwell" is locally pronounced "cowl," to rhyme with "fowl.") From here a waterway channel, hard to see until the canoeist has reached it, leads to S. Sandy Creek, which flows W to Lake Ontario. This trip is about 2 mi one way. It is possible to canoe along the lake shoreline for many miles in either direction.

Caution ✖ Moderate to strong westerly winds will soon produce waves large enough to be extremely dangerous to canoeists. In addition, the current entering Lake Ontario from the marsh area and S. Sandy Creek, while not swift, is very strong and quite dangerous, especially to young children. The shoreline at this point drops off quickly.

A second access point is a state cartop boat launching site, suitable for canoes and kayaks, on S. Sandy Creek at Rt 3. This site has ample parking and portable toilet facilities. It is possible to paddle from here downstream to intersect with the first route described above. At first, large willows overarch the stream and wildflowers grow along the banks. Farther down, this landscape gives way to cattails and marsh grass. At this point the channel turns N, with the barrier beach to the L. Bank swallows nest in the dunes here. This trip is about 1.5 mi, one way.

Takeout Takeout is possible at any of the three access points. The third, a state boat launch site at Lakeview Pond, is reached by turning W from Rt 3 onto Pierrepont Place (sometimes called Pierrepont Rd). There is ample parking, and a gravel road leads down to the launch site. From here the route leads S through Lakeview Pond and a channel through a marsh, intersecting the other two routes. This route is about 2.5 miles long, one way. Landing on the dunes to the W is not advised because of the fragility of the ecosystem. Canoeists unconcerned about this problem may find them-

South Sandy Creek (Lakeview Wildlife Management Area)

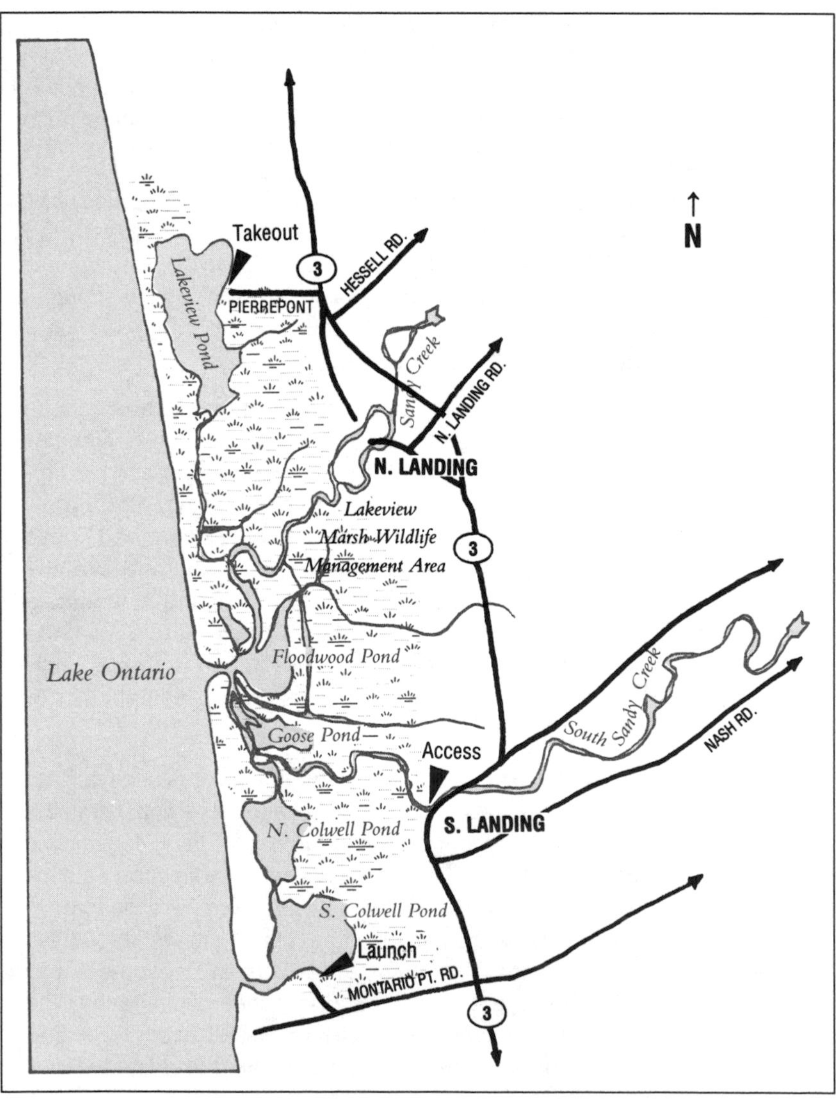

selves ankle deep in poison ivy—the dunes have a defense system.

Obviously, the canoeist may combine any or all of these routes and may wish to explore the ponds and other channels in this area. The accompanying map will be useful in this regard.

French Creek

County: Jefferson

Segment ↕ French Creek Wildlife Area to Village of Clayton (St. Lawrence River)

Length ↔ 5–6 mi

Drop ↘ Negligible

Difficulty ① Class I

Problems ✻ Slight possibility of waves on the St. Lawrence

Maps St. Lawrence, Clayton; DeLorme p 91

Contributor Don Dano

Launch Drive 2 mi W from Clayton on Rt 12E, turn L on Fish Pond Rd. (This becomes Rosiere Rd and is also known locally as Crystal Springs Rd.) One-half mile past Crystal Springs Hotel, take left turn to marsh. Next left is launch area next to bridge, with room for ten vehicles in parking lot.

Description The upper part of the route passes through the Wildlife Management Area. Much of it is a cattail marsh; side creeks enter in two places. Wildlife includes various ducks, shore birds, muskrat, and beaver, but there are, as of this writing (1991), no beaver dams to impede progress.

About halfway to Clayton, on the right side, is a bald rock and several large pine trees. Locally known as Rock-a-Roll-Away, this is a good lunch stop. Further E the marsh and water area widens out to a large mud flat. Soon, ahead and to the L, the town of Clayton and the bridge across French Creek outlet comes into view. Here the stream empties into French Creek Bay.

Takeout The Municipal Pier off Theresa and Mary streets in Clayton affords a convenient takeout point. To reach this from the mouth of the creek, simply paddle N along the shoreline for about one-quarter mile.

Note ☞ Although Grindstone Island, 2 mi away, offers considerable protection to French Creek Bay, strong NW winds produce substantial waves at the mouth of French Creek.

• • • • LAKE ONTARIO DRAINAGE—EAST

Kevin Howells

South Sandy Creek at low water.

Alice Broberg

Owasco Outlet, Barge Canal-Finger Lakes watershed.

Barge Canal-Finger Lakes Watershed
Part VI

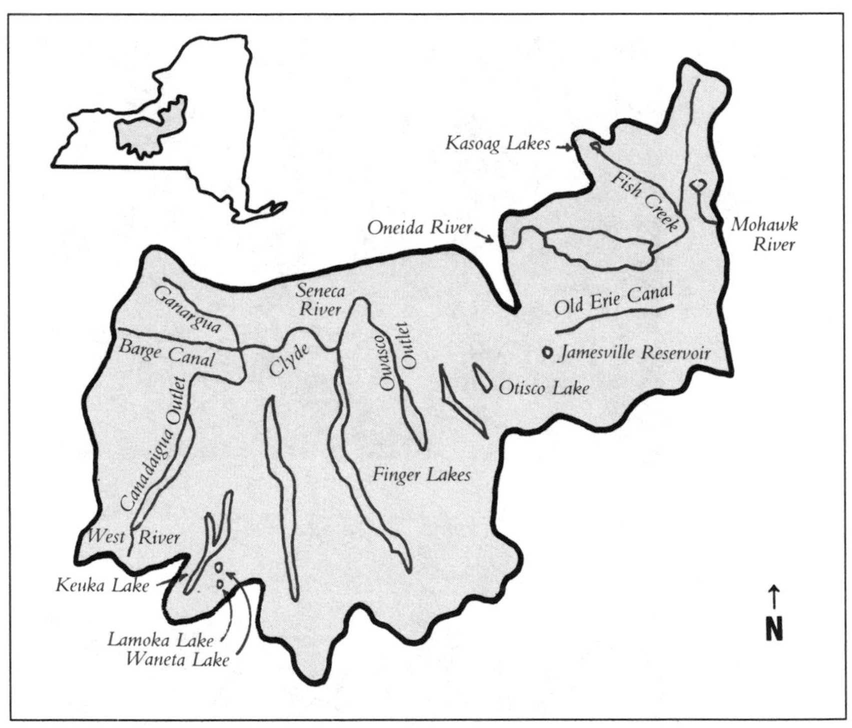

Canoeing the Finger Lakes

The Finger Lakes of New York are the unusual result of glacial action. The last glacier to cover this area scraped out a number of stream valleys, changing them from steep-sided ravines to the characteristic U shape of a glacial valley. As it retreated, it depressed the land to the north so that the streams, augmented by meltwater, flowed N. At the same time, it dropped moraines at the north ends of the valleys, damming the streams. The result was, and still is, a number of long, narrow lakes in central New York: Canandaigua, Keuka, Seneca, Cayuga, Owasco, and many other smaller ones.

All of these lakes are of course canoeable. A few of them, and some of their inlets and outlets, are described on pp 204–224. Not all of the lakes are described in detail here, but the canoeist can assume that those not described are similar to those described; e.g. winds, especially those blowing straight up or down the lake, can be troublesome, as can motorboat traffic. Both can sometimes be avoided by early morning canoeing, and motorboats can sometimes be avoided by canoeing midweek, spring, or fall. The shores of most of the lakes have a great deal of cottage development but some forested or agricultural areas; vineyards are common. State parks and other public launch sites are frequent. The lakes are very beautiful and interesting and well worth canoeing.

New York State Barge Canal

Counties: Various

Segment ↕ Albany to Buffalo (an overview)

Length ↔ About 300 mi

Drop ↘ 570 ft

Difficulty ① Class I

Problems ✻ Locks, commercial and private power boats

Maps Various and numerous

Contributors ✍ Daniel Geist, Mark Freeman, and others

Launch There are hundreds of access points along the canal. Some are state boat launch sites, some are at official canal barge tie-ups, some at town or county parks, some at bridges. It is possible to launch and/or take out at almost every lock. It would be unusual to travel 5 mi along the canal without encountering an access point.

Description ✏ The Erie Canal was begun about 1790 and complëted in 1825. It may well be the most important engineering feat, commercially and historically, ever accomplished in the United States. It greatly facilitated the settling and opening up of the West (anything west of Albany, in those days) created vast fortunes, and gave rise to large cities. It was totally reconstructed in 1918. The entire system, which includes the Erie, Oswego, and Champlain canals and the two divisions of the Cayuga and Seneca Canal, is now officially and prosaically called "The New York State Barge Canal System." Although it is still correct to refer to the segment from Albany to Buffalo as the Erie Canal, it is commonly called simply "the barge canal," although far more pleasure boats than barges travel it.

From the canoeist's point of view, the barge canal offers several attractive possibilities. It is perfectly possible to canoe the canal proper and its water connections from Buffalo to Albany or Montour Falls to Rouses Point or Ithaca to New York City. Most would probably choose a shorter segment of the route. The only difficulties they would encounter would be meetings with tugs and barges, which are now less common than formerly, private power boats of all sizes and descriptions (which are legally required to travel quite slowly), and possible delays at locks, depending on the levels of both water and the New York State budget.

Lake Erie is about 570 ft above mean sea level. Albany is tidal, with a rise and fall of a few feet. The trip between the two points, however, is not downhill all the way. The canal drops in twelve steps to the Onondaga Lake level near Syracuse, then rises 7 ft to Oneida Lake, then 50 ft more to the vicinity of Rome before dropping 420 ft to Albany. The largest single lock in terms of drop, at Little Falls, lets boats down (or lifts them up) 41 ft; the smallest goes up 6 ft.

To make this guide simpler and clearer, we have chosen to regard Tonawanda Creek and its tributaries as draining into Lake Erie. Tonawanda Creek, in its lower reaches, *is* the Barge Canal, with of course little or no current, but before humans interfered with it, it flowed toward Lake Erie and the Niagara River.

Lock tenders may refuse to lock through any boat for safety reasons. They could ask paddlers to leave a canoe to be locked through empty, especially when locking up, when turbulence is greater. This almost never happens, however; they generally are happy to lock canoes and other small boats through, with or without other craft, and delays are uncommon (although in 1991 hours of operation were cut back for budgetary reasons). Most lock tenders will not lock canoes through with barges, for obvious safety reasons, but the likelihood of a canoe and a barge arriving at a lock at the same time is not great, and it is often relatively easy to carry around locks. Most lock areas are kept like, and amount to, public parks. One canoe trip entirely on the canal system is described on p 208–209.

A second attractive possibility is canoeing the old, abandoned Erie Canal segments, which eliminates all three difficulties described above. There are many such segments still canoeable, two of which are discussed on pp 173–180.

Perhaps the most pleasant canoeing possibility created by the construction of the canal is paddling the "loops" of rivers which are partly canalized. Both the original and later construction took advantage of (and took over) many existing waterways in whole or part: the Mohawk River, Wood Creek, Fish Creek, Oneida Lake, the Oswego, Oneida, Clyde and Seneca rivers, and Tonawanda Creek, to name just a few of them. In many cases, cuts made to straighten and shorten the route left delightful water byways, some of which, at least, are only available to canoes, kayaks, and similar non-motorized craft. An astonishing variety of wildlife, especially birds, may be seen on these trips off the canal, sometimes only a few miles from the downtown center of a major city. A few such trips are described in this guide on pp 200–212; many others are possible.

While it would not be especially difficult or dangerous to canoe any part of the canal system with no other guide than a highway map, numerous other aids are available. These include the DeLorme Atlas, appropriate USGS quadrants, pertinent NOAA nautical charts, the New York State Canal

Guide, published by Midlakes Navigation Company Ltd., Skaneateles, N.Y., and any number of maps and publications obtainable free or for a small sum from the New York State Department of Transportation, Waterways Maintenance Division, 5 Governor Harriman State Campus, Albany, NY 12232.

Takeout See LAUNCH above.

Note A bill before the New York State Legislature would make it possible, if the proposition were approved by the voters, for the state to charge tolls on the canal system. What effect this would have, if passed, on canoeing the canal is unknown.

Mohawk River

County: Oneida

Segment Delta Reservoir (spillway outlet) to Rome

Length 8.5 mi

Drop 40 ft

Difficulty Class I (Alternative trip above reservoir Class III or Class IV)

Problems Sharp turns, strong current, possible down trees or limbs

Maps Westernville, Rome; DeLorme pp 76, 77

Contributor Alice Broberg

Launch Access is below the dam and spillway at the S end of Delta Reservoir (Delta Lake), which is reached by driving N from Rome on Rt 46. Turn L onto bridge just below dam. Cross bridge, turn L, stop by the roadside temporarily to unload boats. Parking is available about 50 ft farther on the same road.

Note Expert whitewater paddlers sometimes launch above the reservoir during the spring run-off, either at the hamlet of Hillside or farther down at Northwestern, for a wild ride through riffles and standing waves, around sharp turns and tree branches. From Northwestern to Delta Lake the river drops 100 ft in 3 mi. This trip can be done only at very high water levels and should be done only by experts who are properly prepared, skilled, and equipped.

Delta Lake itself is canoeable, with the usual lake problems at times of wind waves and motorboats. There are two state boat launch sites on the lake, and swimming is possible at Delta Lake State Park Beach.

Description The Mohawk, second in New York State only to the Hudson in historic and commercial importance, rises on the Tug Hill Plateau, flows roughly S to Rome, then turns E for over 100 miles to empty into the Hudson just N of Albany. Unfortunately for canoeists but fortunately for commerce, from Rome to Albany most of it coincides with the Barge Canal. From Delta Reservoir to Rome, the Mohawk is a narrow, fast fun run.

The launch is into a narrow eddy, after which the paddler should be prepared for fast current and low-hanging branches, which have been cut to make canoe passage possible but tend to grow back. After a sharp L turn at the fish hatchery, the stream passes under the Rt 46 bridge and moves rapidly straight ahead. A sharp R turn leads to some riffles, a narrow, rocky channel, then wider riffles. At this point, and from here to takeout, the shoreline, actually a Rome city park, is clean and wooded.

Takeout The recommended takeout is on the grassy shoreline adjacent to George Staley Junior High School. There is a parking lot behind the school, but cars can be brought around closer to the river for loading. The school is on E. Bloomfield St, Rome, 7 blocks E of Black River Blvd. On weekends and other occasions when school is not in session, it is permissible to use the school parking lot.

Note ☞ Between Rome and the Hudson River, numerous short and some longer stretches of the old river loop away from the canal and back, offering attractive trips to recreational boaters. Access sites and lock parks and other facilities are maintained by the New York State departments of Transportation and Environmental Conservation, as well as cities and towns along the route.

Old Erie Canal

Counties: Onondaga, Madison

Segment ↕ DeWitt to Canastota

Length ↔ 17 mi

Drop ↘ Negligible

Difficulty ① Class I

Problems ✻ Debris including possible down trees

Maps Syracuse E, Manlius, Canastota; DeLorme pp 75, 76

Contributors ✍ Lawrence W. Keefe, Alice Broberg, Mark Freeman

Launch There are numerous access points along the Old Erie Canal. At most bridges it is possible to launch or take out, but it almost always involves a short steep carry up a bank. Between Syracuse and Canastota no road parallels the canal for very long; finding all the bridges by car requires a good map and good map-reading skills.

This trip begins at the westernmost possible point. It is reached by taking Erie Blvd E in Syracuse and turning L on Kinne Rd, which goes over I-481. Just before this bridge, Butternut Drive comes in R from the S; just after the bridge it leaves Kinne Rd headed N. About .1 mi N on Butternut from this turn is a public parking area R with space for some fifteen cars. Canoes may be carried a short distance to the canal, which emerges from a culvert at this point.

Description This is the old canal, no longer in use commercially nor usable by large power boats. It is easy and flat, an ideal spot for children or beginners to have their first canoeing experience. Although the gradient is almost nil, there is a slight easterly current. Its entire length from Syracuse to Fort Bull, 37 mi E, including old towpaths and land on either side, comprises Old Erie Canal State Park. There are occasional obstacles and debris, especially near the eastern terminus, and although there is never any real difficulty, many of the bridges passed under will give the canoeist a new appreciation of the old canal cry: "Low bridge! Everybody down!" For most of the route paddlers have the company of joggers and bikers on paths beside the canal.

From the launch, a dozen yards of paddling brings the canoeist into a narrow limestone aqueduct over Butternut Creek, the first of three streams the canal passes over. The route passes through wide Cedar Bay, which has water lilies, yellow iris, and a resident great blue heron. The first of several Canal Museums is L here.

After passing under the Burdick St bridge, the canal goes

over Limestone Creek at the 2.25-mi mark. About 2.5 mi farther, the route goes under the Green Lakes State Park footbridge. The park, just S of here, offers camping, swimming, and other activities, but there is no direct water access from the canal to the lakes. Six miles from launch, the route reaches the Kirkville Rd bridge. This is a possible access point with good parking, but Pools Brook Rd access point 1 mi farther is much better. It is reached by car, not easily, as follows: From the intersection of Rts 5 and 257 in the center of Fayetteville, take 257 N 1.8 mi to Rt 290. Follow 290 NE 2.75 mi to Kirkville Rd; take Kirkville N, crossing the canal, 1 mi to Pools Brook Rd. Follow the twists and turns of Pools Brook Rd E, then S, recrossing the canal, 1.8 mi to Andrus Rd. Turn L on Andrus and proceed .3 mi to a state launch area with parking and picnic facilities. A slightly simpler route to reach this spot was impossible in June 1991 because a bridge was out. From the canoeist's point of view, the access point is R at a widewater (the remains of an old turning basin). This is a popular lunch stop; sybarites sometimes have a luxurious picnic brought out by car from Syracuse.

Passing the reconstruction of an 1820s canal building, paddlers reach Chittenango-Lakeport Rd, 3.5 mi from Pools Brook Rd, where the local American Legion Post has created an attractive access point at a pleasant wooded part of the canal. Joggers and bikers are not so numerous from here on. Passing under several bridges, a long straight stretch leads to Canastota, about 6 miles farther. Canastota has a Canal Museum and other historic preservations.

Takeout It used to be possible to canoe right through Canastota, passing under streets through large culverts, but this is no longer true. The first bridge reached in Canastota is Main St, which is distinguished by a low steel rail which at

Old Erie Canal • DeWitt to Canastota

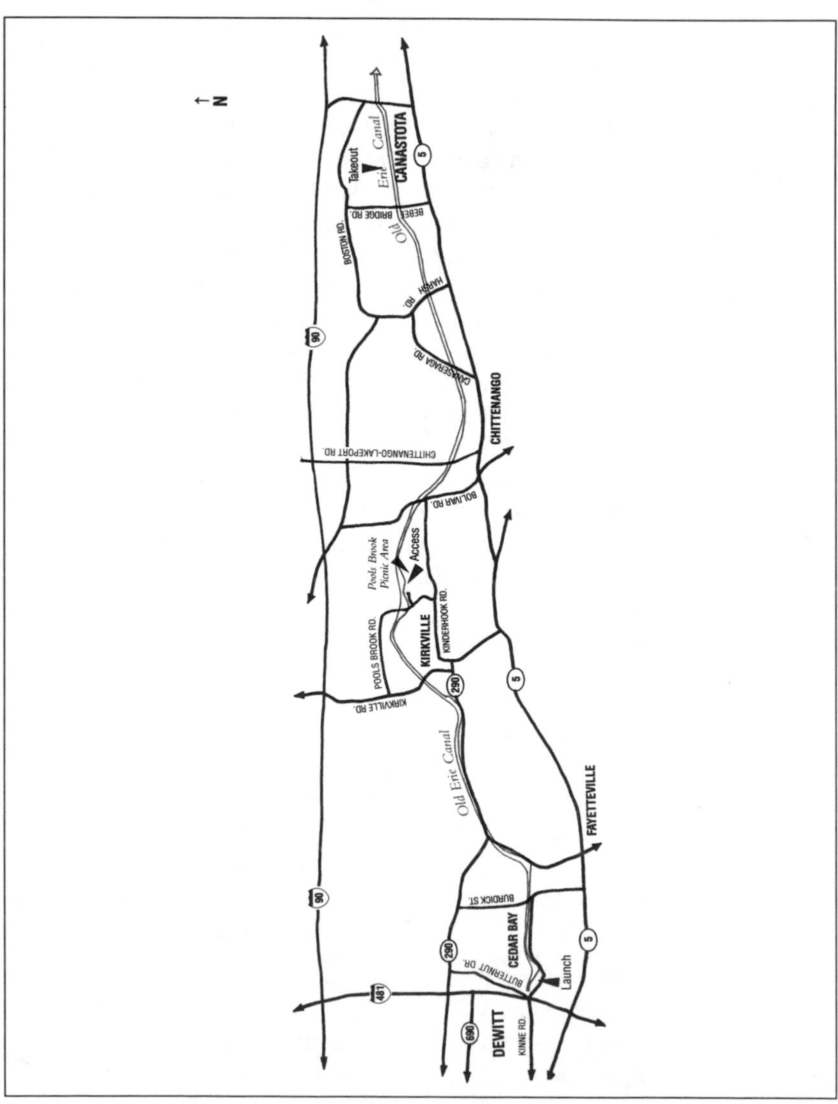

some water levels makes it impossible to go on. If the canoeist feels he can get under this, the next access point is much better. If not, takeout is L well upstream of the bridge.

If the low steel rail can be passed, a short city block farther are two culverts: Now the canal disappears underground for about a block, emerging at Diamond St. An easy takeout is L of the culverts: there is seldom any appreciable current to contend with here. The street paralleling the canal L in the town is State St, which quickly becomes Canal St. There is plenty of parking in town all around this area.

Old Erie Canal

Counties: Madison, Oneida

Segment ↕ Canastota to New London

Length ↔ 13 mi

Drop ↘ Negligible

Difficulty ① Class I

Problems ✻ Debris including down trees, low water in places, low bridges

Maps Canastota, Oneida, Sylvan Beach, Verona; DeLorme p 76

Contributors Lawrence W. Keefe, Alice Broberg, Mark Freeman

Launch In Canastota access is possible at Diamond St on river R downstream. (Downstream is toward New London; upstream is toward Syracuse.) (See preceding entry.)

Description The easternmost sections of the Old Erie Canal grow progressively shallower and more strewn with debris, but the trip is still worthwhile historically if for no other reason. In early 1991 a break in an aqueduct which carries the canal over a creek near Durhamville had been temporarily repaired, but there was still some leakage and the water level was quite low, making the trip much less pleasant. In general, this stretch is quite unlike the part of the canal near Syracuse, where joggers, bikers, and paddlers are the rule rather than the exception. While placing a car for the expected end of the trip, canoeists should check water level and impediments for themselves to the degree possible.

From Canastota the canal trends NE. Canal Rd (Canal St on some signs) parallels the canal through residential streets and cultivated fields, offering access at several points. At N. Court St, N of Wampsville, 2 mi from launch, there are three bridges in rapid succession. The first, the old bridge, is on a dead-end road, and access is possible upstream on the R. Neither access nor parking are terribly good. The new bridges carry twin lanes over the canal; even at low water it is necessary to duck for quite a while, and it is barely possible to see light at the end of the tunnel.

Two more miles of lightly wooded scenery bring the canoeist to the I-90 bridges, and in another mile Durhamville is reached. Here the canal turns N and even a trifle W. From here to the end of the trip Rt 46 parallels the canal. This is an open, attractive stretch, although down trees and other debris and shallow water may be encountered. At Rt 31, about 7 mi from launch, access is possible, but a much better possibility exists at a highway rest area with picnic tables on the east side of Rt 46 a short distance N of 31.

Old Erie Canal • Canastota to New London

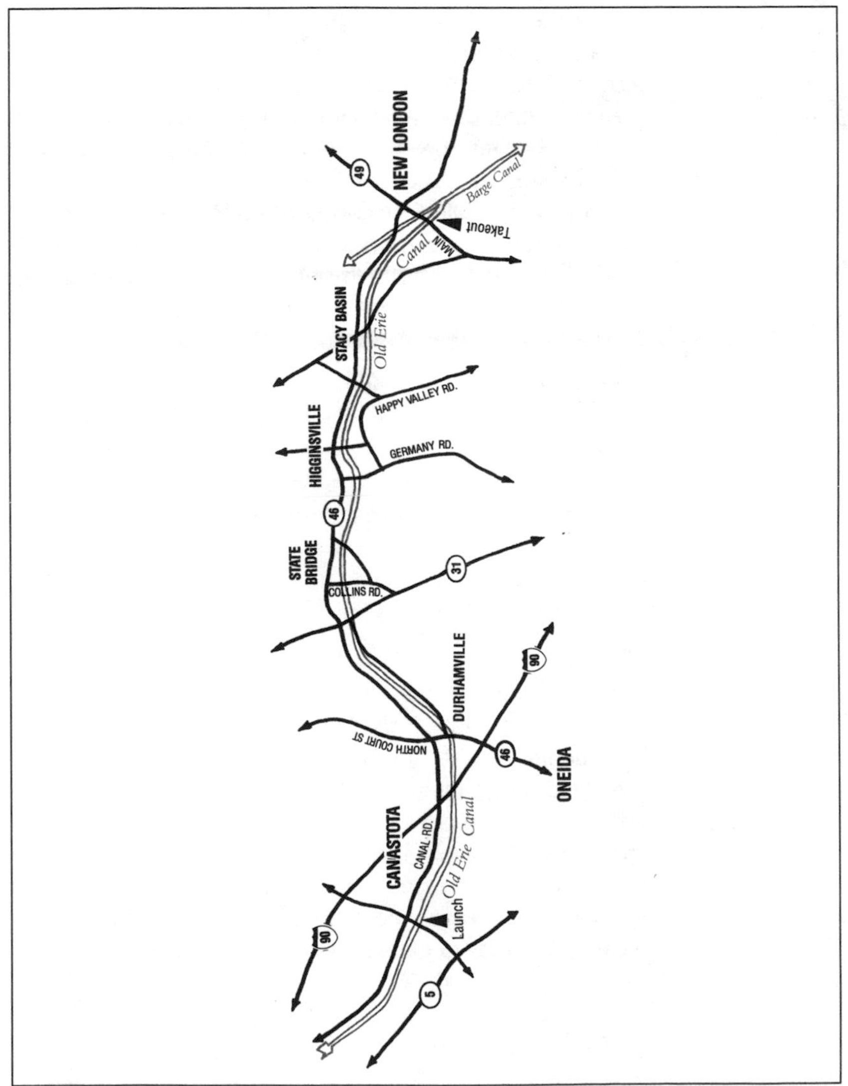

Now the canal begins a gradual bend to the E. There are numerous bridges. At about the 11-mi point at Stacy Basin, paddlers get a ground level view of open farmland, after which trees again predominate for the next 2 mi to New London. Although a developed trail for bikers and hikers follows the old towpath through most of Old Erie Canal State Park, it does not exist in a couple of sections between Durhamville and New London. Problems with debris and low water, while never insurmountable, grow worse as New London is approached.

Takeout It is possible to take out at the Main St bridge, the only bridge in New London, across the road from Satch's Tavern. New London is not so large a community that this is difficult to find. Parking is also possible in this area, but the canoeist will want to scout the takeout carefully. Access is to the old towpath L a short distance upstream of the bridge. Below this bridge the old canal drains into the New York State Barge Canal. This section is totally impassable.

Note Brochures published by New York State describing the Old Erie Canal State Park do not make it clear that the 5-mi segment of the old canal linking the barge canal with Erie Canal Village just W of Rome no longer exists, but this is the case. It is well worth the short drive on Rts 46 and 49 from New London to see a reconstructed village on a short reconstructed canal segment and take a ride on an old horse-drawn packet boat, but it is not possible to canoe there or to canoe after you get there.

Kasoag Lakes ("The Place")

County: Oswego

Segment First, Second, Third, and Fourth lakes; Shingle Mill Creek, Green Pond (Fifth Lake)

Length 4 mi round trip

Drop Negligible

Difficulty Class I

Problems Beaver dam, shallow culvert

Maps Williamstown; DeLorme p 75

Contributor Alice Broberg

Launch There are just two possible access points to this group of lakes. The first is Kasoag Lake Park, which is reached by taking Rt 13 to Williamstown and County Rt 30, thence N to where it crosses the outlet of the lakes, the source of the West Branch of Fish Creek. The park offers an easy launch, as well as delightful swimming, at a sandy beach. There is adequate parking. A short distance further along 30 is another possible access point at a grassy area next to a white frame building (the old hotel). Parking here is limited to the shoulder of Rt 30. Access is not permitted anywhere else; all lakefront property is privately owned and access to the lakeshore is limited to residents and visitors.

Description This general area is called "The Place" because, in earlier times, various tribes of Native Americans used it as a resting place on trading trips. One obvious canoe route from

Lake Ontario to the Mohawk River would pass through here, and Kasoag Lakes would be a natural stopping place. This is a beautiful group of small lakes, spring-fed, shallow, comprising about 100 acres with generally wooded shores as well as many summer camps and year-round homes. The moderately steep shores are lined with big hemlocks, beech and maple trees. The lake level is seldom affected by rain, and at the height of summer paddlers can enjoy the shaded channels. Beaver, muskrat, loons, ducks and herons are among the wildlife to be seen, and the fishin' is easy.

The route begins by exploring the east shoreline, a series of narrow, distinct channels classified as separate lakes but connected by a water corridor. After exploring the last of these channels, the canoeist should paddle ahead into a current coming from the R, through a passage around a steep peninsula topped by a vintage summer cottage. This landmark can be seen from either side of the peninsula. After passing through a culvert under a private road, the paddler turns L into Shingle Mill Creek.

A moderately difficult beaver dam may be encountered here, demonstrating the remoteness of the stream, which leads to Green Pond. While all of the completely wooded shores of the pond are posted, there is no objection to canoeing Green Pond or fishing from a canoe there.

Returning, the route is retraced to the point at which it is possible to travel along the west shoreline, where there is a modern year-round residence quite close to the water's edge, as well as many little wooded channels, water plants, and shoreline vegetation. The route returns along the south shore to the launch point. There may be some narrow channels along this route which are easier to negotiate in a small solo canoe.

Takeout Takeout is at the launch point.

West Branch, Fish Creek

County: Oneida

Segment ↕ Westdale Marsh

Length ↔ 8 mi or more (round trip), depending on conditions

Drop ↘ Negligible

Difficulty ① Class I

Problems ✻ Winding, narrow stream, false channels, beaver dams

Maps Westdale; DeLorme p 76

Contributors ✍ Alice Broberg, Ron Schlie, Kevin Howells

Launch A large state-maintained access point with plenty of parking and steps leading down to the water's edge is on a reservoir created by a dam in the hamlet of Westdale. This spot is reached by taking Rt 69 18 mi NW from Rome to its intersection with Rt 13 in Camden, then continuing NW 5 mi on 13 to Westdale. The launch point is about 100 yds NE of 13 on the east side of Cemetery Rd S of the bridge.

Note ☞ It is possible for a determined paddler in a small solo canoe or kayak to launch into the West Branch below the dam at Kasoag Lake (see preceding entry) and travel through brush, strainers, and beaver dams on the narrow winding stream 5 mi to Williamstown. A correspondent says of this trip: "Not recommended. Not paddleable by a sane individual. (I did it.)" At Williamstown such a paddler could carry around a small dam and continue, if there were plenty of water, through similar conditions, as well as marshes, to Westdale. The Indians did it.

West Branch, Fish Creek • Westdale Launch Sites

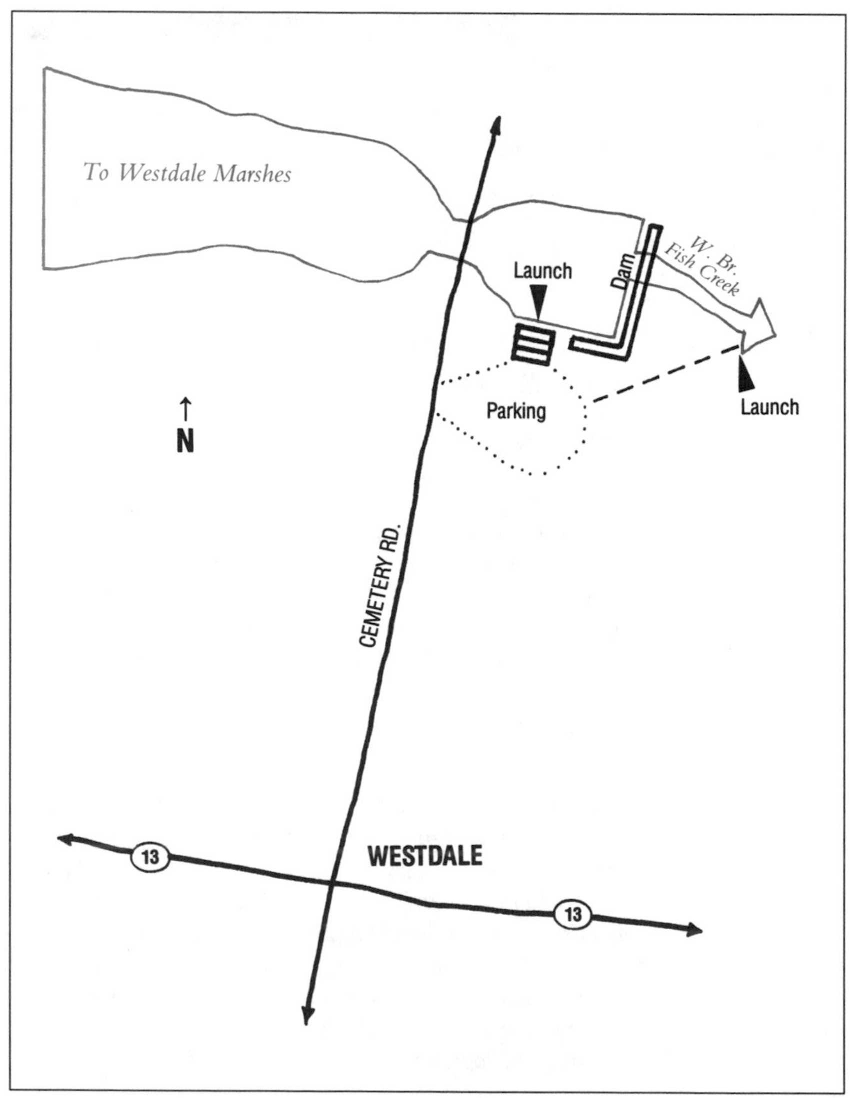

Description The West Branch of Fish Creek flows out of the Kasoag Lake complex and travels about 30 mi to its confluence with the East Branch, meandering even more than most small streams enroute. It was part of an important trade route linking Lake Ontario with the Mohawk-Hudson watershed, used by Native Americans before the coming of the white man. It contrasts astonishingly with the East Branch. (See p 193.) The latter is a wild whitewater ride, one of the most challenging in New York. The West Branch offers primarily moving water and occasional easy Class I rapids through wilderness scenery which resembles the Adirondacks.

After launch, paddlers should proceed upstream, keeping to the main channel. At choice points, this is often to the left. In many places, observing current on the stream bottom will help. There are several cottages and homes for the first .5 mi, above which the stream resembles a remote Adirondack waterway. About 1.5 mi from launch a right-hand channel leads to Gifford Lake, which offers good fishing in a wilderness setting. The main route continues to be L, against current growing stronger and around many bends. This is good fishing, birding, and wildlife backcountry with clear moving water which is canoeable from ice-out to freeze-up. About 2.5 mi from launch the route passes under Rt 13. Canoeists can continue for several more miles depending on their strength, skill, and determination, and that of the current. The trip often ends at wooded high ground about 6 mi from launch.

Takeout Return to launch point for takeout.

West Branch, Fish Creek

County: Oneida

Segment ↕ Westdale to Camden

Length ↔ 9.5 mi

Drop ↘ 25 ft

Difficulty ② Class I

Problems Strainers, down trees

Maps Westdale, Camden W; DeLorme p 76

Contributors Alice Broberg, Ron Schlie, Kevin Howells

Launch From Westdale parking lot, carry a short distance to launch below dam, following trails made by fishermen. (See previous entry.)

Description This is an exciting trip at H level or better, but nearly impossible with less water. Even with sufficient water, paddlers may experience some shoals as well as the usual sweepers and strainers. The route passes through pine and hardwood forest, along with lowlands where alders and willows predominate. Current is usually moderate. In the first half of the trip the stream twists and turns and the paddler must be alert for obstacles around blind corners. From the Rt 13 bridge, 7 mi from launch, the stream moves more directly. In 1991, construction work on this bridge necessitated a short carry. The trip includes runs, riffles, and flatwater.

Takeout About 9.5 mi from launch the stream passes under an unnamed road. This bridge, the next after Rt 13, is the recommended takeout. It is reached by taking Rt 13 NW from

Camden 1.75 mi to a McDonald's restaurant, which marks the turn. The access point is about .5 mi S of the intersection.

Note ☞ It is possible, and sometimes fun, to canoe farther, but the next mile or two into and through Camden is a steeplechase of dams and bridges with repeated takeouts and relaunches around dams and other obstacles, interspersed with fast water, sometimes in a gorge. It should be scouted extensively with attention given to takeout and relaunch points. At most water levels this stretch only occasionally approaches Class II, but for those who wish to canoe the creek farther the best option is probably a car carry from here to the sewage treatment plant. (See next entry.)

West Branch, Fish Creek

County: Oneida

Segment ↕ Camden to Oswego Rd

Length ↔ 15 mi

Drop ↘ 90 ft

Difficulty ② Class I above McConnellsville, Class II below

Problems ✻ Strainers, particularly at blind corners, a dam to be portaged

Maps Camden E, Lee Center; DeLorme p 76

Contributors ✍ Ron Schlie, Alice Broberg, Kevin Howells

Launch A popular launch point is at the Camden Sewage Treatment Plant, which is off Rt 69 about 1 mi SE of the center of

Camden. An access road runs SE to the plant here. Parking is available where this road takes a sharp turn R. Launch is river L just below where Mad River enters the West Branch of Fish Creek. It is necessary to carry boats across barbed wire; planks are permanently laid over the wire for this purpose.

Description Rt 13 parallels the stream from Camden to McConnellsville; access is possible at almost any crossroad. The first 1.5 mi from launch is meandering, with occasional swampy terrain; then Brewer Rd, another popular access point, is reached. Below this bridge, a mild rapid can be avoided, if desired, by keeping L. From Brewer Rd to Buell Rd, 3.25 mi, the current is slow-moving and the banks are fern-covered. Wood ducks and mergansers are often seen here or elsewhere on this trip. The current picks up after the route passes under an old RR trestle bridge. Several side channels R should be avoided, since they are likely to present the typical small stream problems of down trees and sharp curves. Right after the faster water, a good place to stop for lunch is at a sandy beach L just before the Trestle Rd bridge, which is 6 mi from launch.

From here to McConnellsville was formerly flatwater paddling, but part of the old wooden dam in McConnellsville was carried away in the spring of 1991, making this stretch moving water and a more pleasant paddle but replacing the attractive fern-lined reservoir with a muddy bank and a jumble of rocks and logs. Whether or not the dam will be rebuilt is unknown at this writing.

The takeout for the carry around the broken dam is immediately after the Depot Rd bridge; paddlers must go under the bridge well L to be ready for the takeout, and since there is room for only one or two canoes at a time, others must be well spread out upriver. A large white house atop a hill above the new bridge and the sight and sound of the Harden Furniture Company (the owner of the dam) are indications that the dam is near. Boats are carried down large concrete steps to be relaunched below the dam.

At H level or better, the paddler will encounter easy Class I rapids and wide curves around a trailer park as the trip continues to the confluence with the East Branch, 4 mi farther. This section should not be run by novices unaccompanied by more experienced paddlers. Two miles below the dam the channel splits into several parts. The main channel is R. Where the stream makes a quick S curve strainers are again a possibility; an experienced individual or pair should go through first to check for obstructions. This section can often be avoided by taking one of the shallow side channels L.

The second bridge after McConnellsville is Blossvale Rd, a possible access point. About .25 mi from this bridge the East Branch enters L. At H water levels this section can be turbulent and should be run very carefully; canoeists have been known to decide to line down. There are strong crosscurrents; the observer can sometimes see mounds of water higher than the general level where the two streams come together. The East Branch joins the West in a delta with multiple channels and, except at flood stage, there are often one or more gravel islands at the junction. It is important for less experienced paddlers to get over to the left side quickly at the confluence. The more powerful current R can sweep the unwary into down trees at a turn just below here. From here to Oswego Rd, 2.25 mi farther, Fish Creek is fast-moving and divides around a few islands, but obstructions are rare; the current wipes them out. It is a smooth river curving through high bluffs occupied by myriads of bank swallows. Deer, ospreys, grouse, and ducks are among the wildlife to be seen on this part of the trip. It is secluded and

West Branch, Fish Creek • Camden Launch Site

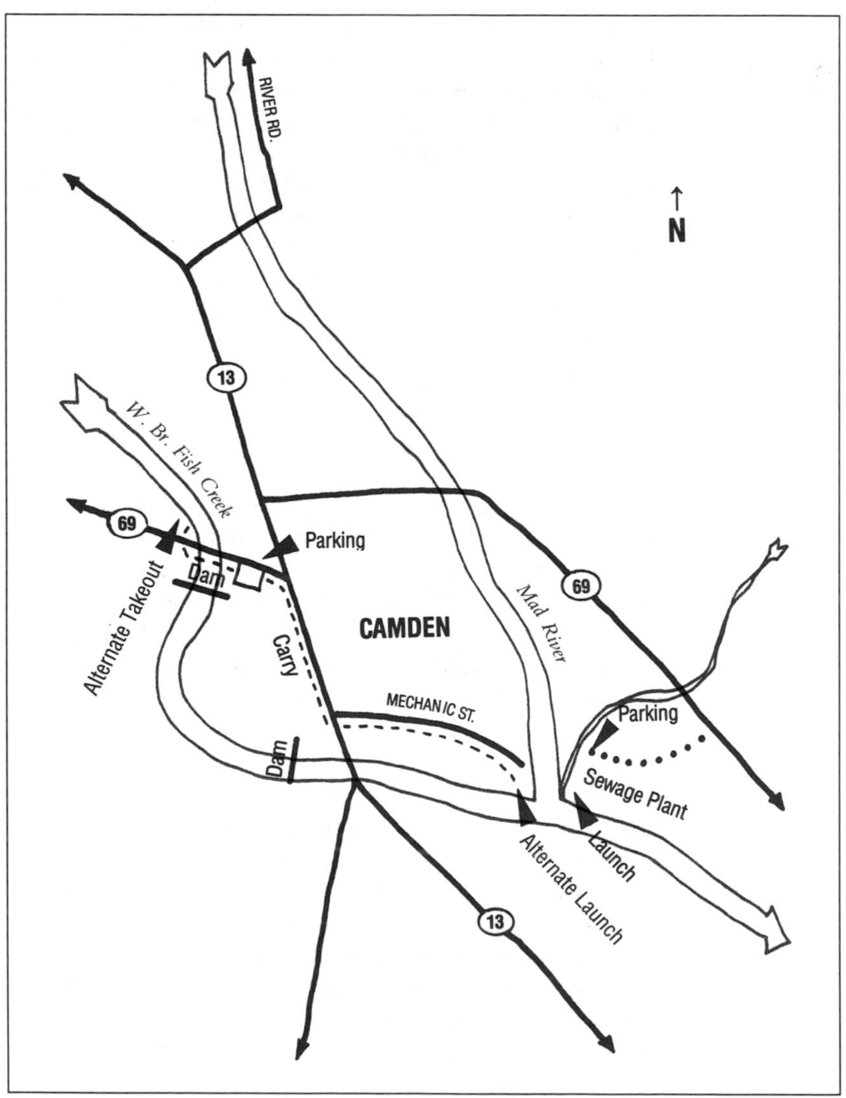

West Branch, Fish Creek • McConnellsville Dam

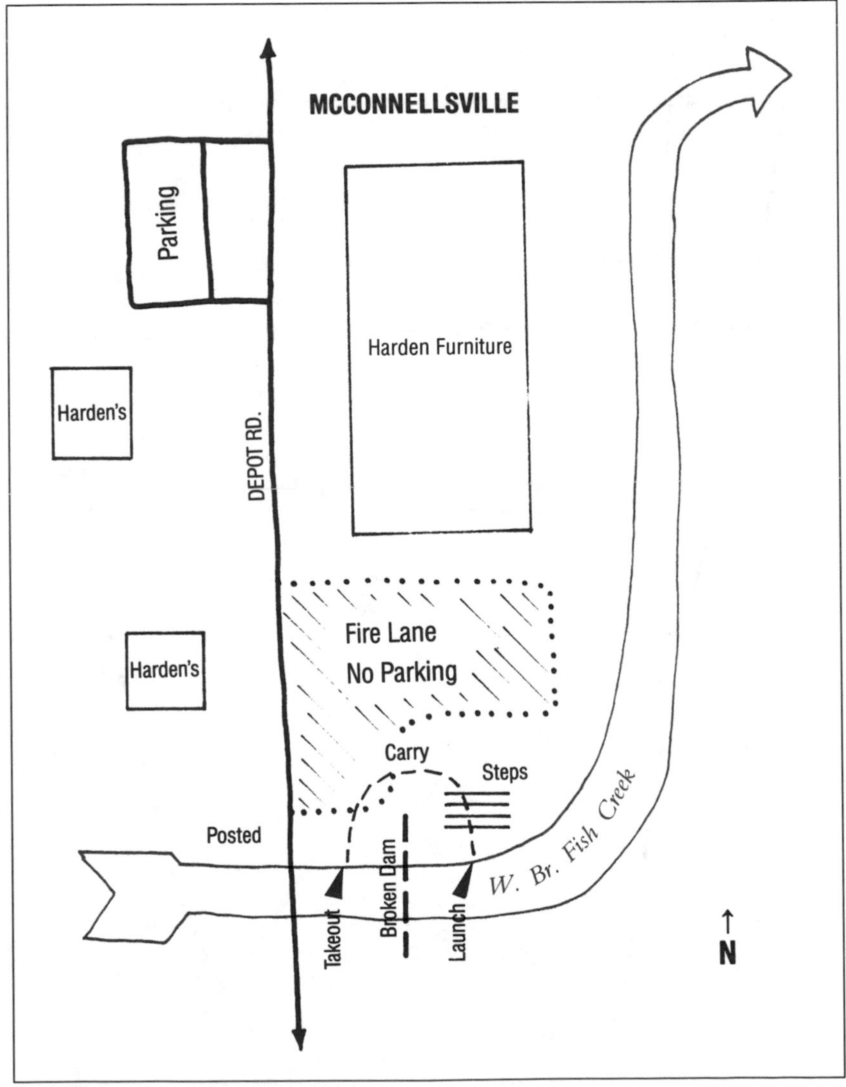

West Branch, Fish Creek • Oswego Road Takeout

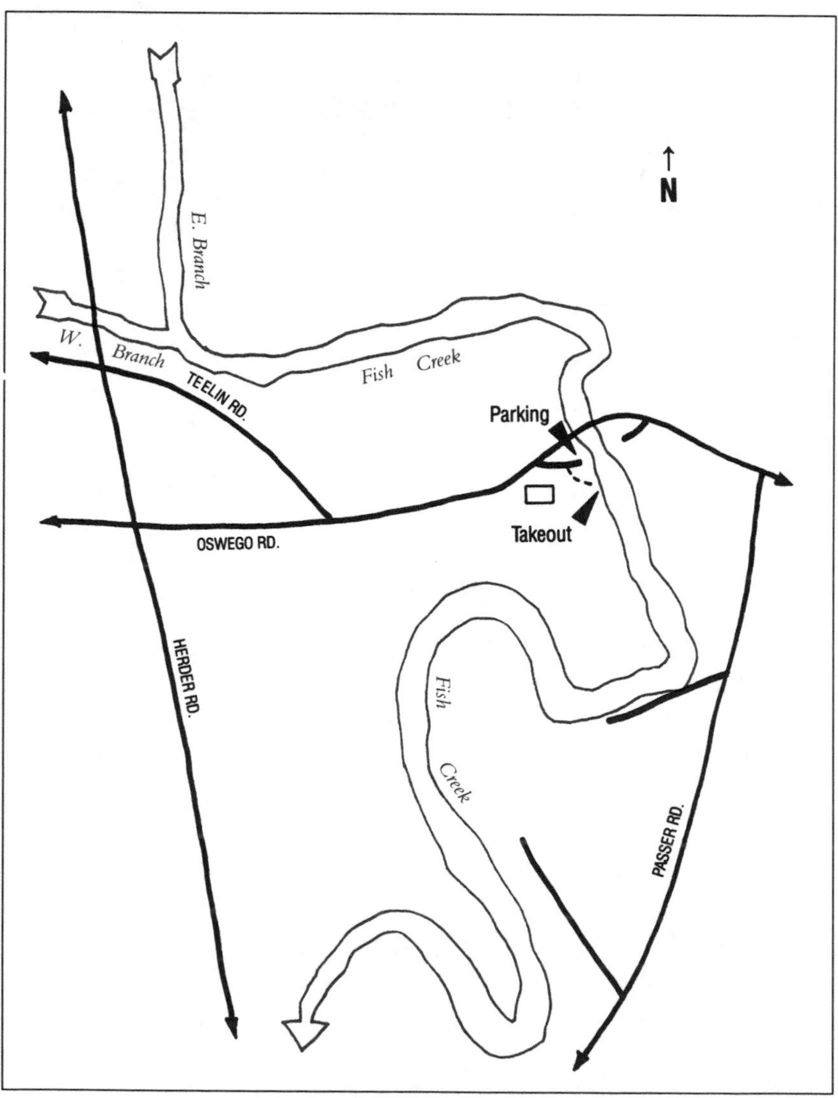

forested at first, with more signs of civilization as the takeout is approached.

Takeout This trip ends just below Oswego Rd bridge. The fact that this used to be the Oswego Log Rd offers an interesting insight into the history of the area. Takeout is R downstream of the bridge at the dead end of an old side road with parking for a number of cars. Canoes must be carried up a steep bank about 15 ft high, but this is a very popular access point. This spot is reached by taking Rt 69 from Rome 6.5 mi NW to Humaston Rd, turning L onto Humaston for 2.5 mi to Oswego Rd, and traveling NW about 1 mi to the bridge. Just after crossing the bridge, turn L on the side road which led to the former bridge. A Ford dealership marks the turn onto the side road. It is also possible to take out L at this access point since there are dead-end roads on either side which formerly led to the old bridge.

East Branch, Fish Creek

County: Oneida

Segment Yorkland Rd to Taberg (Blossvale Rd)

Length 9 mi

Drop 500 ft

Difficulty Class III verging on Class IV

Problems 2 dams, one of which is unrunnable, heavy rapids

Maps Point Rock, Lee Center, Camden E; DeLorme p 76

Contributor Kevin Howells

Launch The highest feasible access point for the East Branch of Fish Creek is on river L just downstream of the Yorkland Rd bridge. Parking is possible here on the north side of the road. To reach Yorkland Rd, turn off Main St (Cty Rt 285) in Taberg onto Coal Hill Rd and drive N 7.5 mi. Turn E on Yorkland and drive .7 mi to launch point.

This run can only be made at MH or better water level, 2 ft on the gauge on the downstream L bridge abutment at Taberg. Mountain Sports (315-896-4421) will provide information by telephone about water levels. There are two bridges at Taberg; the gauge is on the upstream one.

Description This is one of the two or three most difficult and challenging whitewater runs described in this guide. It should not be attempted except by very skilled paddlers, in groups, with proper equipment. The reporter says that it can be canoed in an open boat but only by a highly skilled and experienced paddler in a solo boat at levels well below flood stage. Tandem paddlers with similar skills would probably succeed at levels below 2.5 ft. The reader should bear in mind that, according to the International Scale, Class IV water is "generally not possible for open canoes." Classifications of rapids are arbitrary and subjective, and what some paddlers can do in an open canoe, others can't.

Until Palmer Rd is reached, the route passes through a steep-walled gorge with limited access, and when the water is high enough, it is usually cold snowmelt. It is understandably a very popular trip with kayakers and other whitewater enthusiasts.

The run begins with mild rapids until Point Rock and Point Rock Creek are passed at the .75 mi mark. Below this are some good surfing waves. Many rapids form at bends, with the heavier waves on the outside of the turn at the gorge wall. Those wishing to avoid the heavier water should ferry to the inside of the bend. In early spring, which is when the run is usually made, there are huge icicles on the gorge walls, which DO occasionally fall. The creek is narrow enough that strainers can also be a problem.

At the 3.75-mi point Fall Brook enters R; it is worth pausing to gaze up this stream at the most spectacular of the many falls along the route. About 5 mi from launch, the Rome Water Supply dam can be seen ahead as the paddler rounds a bend. At this point the stream has dropped about 250 ft for an average gradient of 50 ft or more per mi. The dam is totally unrunnable; takeout is L just upstream of the dam. The space is small, so each boat must hold back until the preceding boat is out of the water. It is a wise precaution to set a throw rope here.

This is a good place for lunch, but it is unwise to spend too much time staring at the lethal-looking hydraulic below the dam. The carry L around the dam is short, easy, and obvious. It is possible to start the trip by launching here, but cars must be parked at the corner of Boyd Rd and Streun Rd and the carry is about .5 mi. All of the land along the access road is posted, but the road itself is commonly used by paddlers and fishermen.

One-third of a mile below the dam are some excellent surfing waves, and at 5.75 mi from launch is a wide rapid with several souse holes, followed quickly by a major hole R. At levels over 3 ft this hole should be avoided by all paddlers. At 6 mi, around a sweeping R turn, is a large powerful hole known to paddlers as Hotel California. (" 'Cause you can check out, but you can never leave.") This must be passed carefully on the R; that is, the paddler leaves it on his left. About .33 mi farther are numerous smaller holes all across the river which must be dodged. Palmer Rd bridge, a good takeout for those who only want to run the gorge section, is about 6.5 mi from launch.

East Branch, Fish Creek • Yorkland Rd to Taberg (Blossvale Rd)

Between Palmer Rd and Taberg are many strainers. Below Palmer Rd, the route passes to the L of an island, after which the paddler must ferry R quickly to avoid a ledge. Then follow some good surfing waves, after which the river splits into two main channels. The recommended route is R.

At about 7.5 mi the river divides again. The right channel is narrow with little water and many strainers. The left provides a set of small surfing waves followed by a Class II rapid culminating in a water main with a cement apron, forming essentially a low dam. At 2.5 ft or lower, this can be run on the right edge, but at higher levels it should be run at the center. One-half mile below this dam is the town of Taberg, with two bridges. Takeout is possible R above the first bridge. From here to the recommended takeout is 1 mi of delightful class III to IV rapids with waves and holes.

Takeout About 9.25 mi from launch, the bank becomes low enough to land and carry canoes to Blossvale Rd, which parallels the stream W and is close at this point. Taberg is 10 mi NW of Rome on Rt 69; Blossvale Rd is the first L after the bridge; the takeout point is .75 mi from the turn.

Note Canoeing from here to the junction with the West Branch, 3 mi downstream, is similar to what has come before. A solid Class III rapid is immediately below the takeout; thereafter the rapids gradually diminish to fast-moving water. A paddler continuing downstream would probably take out at Oswego Rd. (See p 193.)

Fish Creek

County: Oneida

Segment Oswego Rd to Oneida Lake

Length 10 mi

Drop 10 ft

Difficulty Class I

Problems Motorboats and possible wind waves on lower section

Maps Camden E, Lee Center, Verona, Sylvan Beach; DeLorme p 76

Contributors Ron Schlie, Alice Broberg, Kevin Howells

Launch Access is near the Oswego Rd bridge. (See previous entry, p 193.)

Description This section is not recommended when the wind is westerly and more than a zephyr, since the waterway is much wider and more open than it is higher up. There is still some current with an occasional riffle and shallow section, but basically this is a good stretch to run with a spinning rod in one hand and a paddle in the other. Just below launch are scenic clay bluffs and several wild loops. The new Rt 49 bridge, which replaces the old Herder Rd bridge, is 3 mi from launch and a possible alternate launch point, but parking is better at the recommended launch.

Fish Creek is 60 ft wide here, full and flat with occasional gentle riffles, meandering through fields and meadows. Campgrounds, camps, and marinas line the lower stretches of the creek. The closer canoeists get to the Barge Canal and Oneida Lake, the more they should beware of motorboat traffic, which does not always slow down, and wind waves. Motorboats are fewer before Memorial Day.

Fish Creek • Fish Creek Takeout

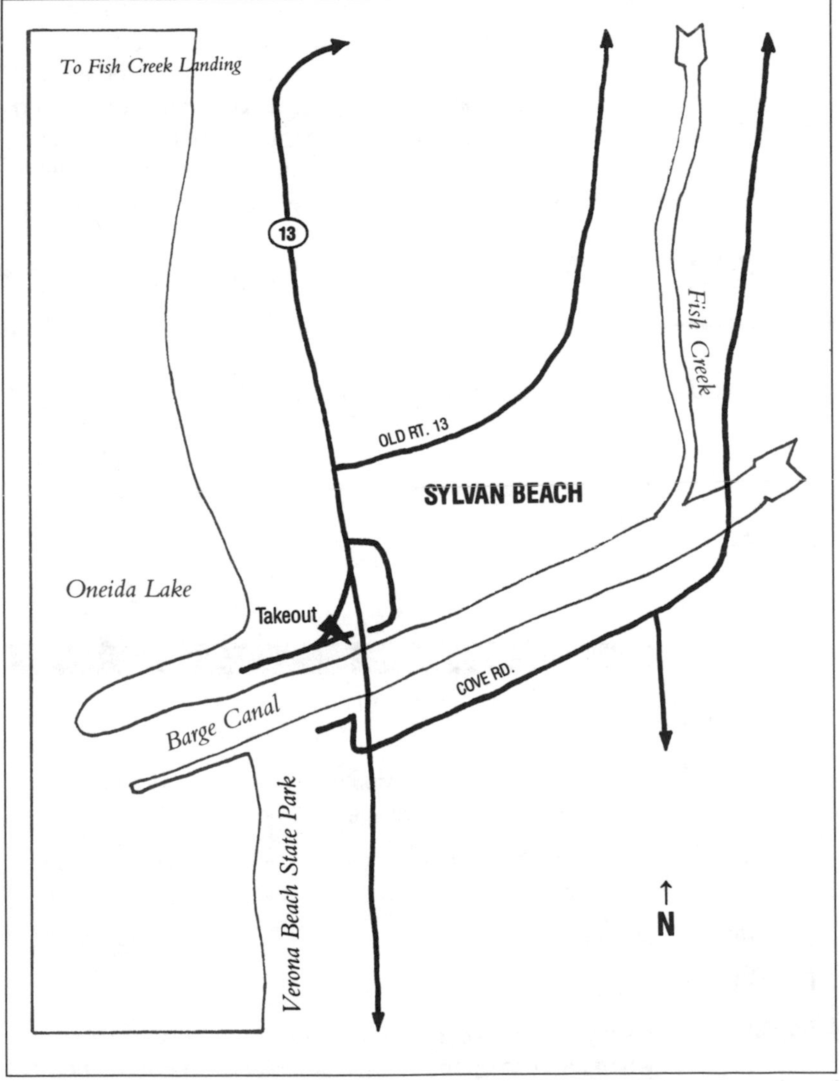

Takeout There is a state launch site R under the Rt 13 bridge in Sylvan Beach, with the usual parking facilities. Steps in the wall of the canal allow canoe access. This is a good access point on a calm day before Memorial Day; however, bearing in mind the problems cited above, it may be better to look for road pull-offs along Cove Rd and in the nearby hamlet of Fish Creek Landing and exit there if boat traffic is expected to be heavy or if it is windy.

Caution While all lakes can be dangerous to canoe in moderate to high winds, Oneida Lake has a particularly bad reputation in this regard.

Camping There are two commercial campgrounds in Fish Creek Landing and one in Sylvan Beach. Verona Beach State Park, about 1 mi S of Sylvan Beach, offers most of the usual facilities, including camping, but does not have a boat launch site.

Oneida River/Oswego River

Counties: Oswego, Onondaga

Segment 1. Caughdenoy Dam to Mouth of Oneida (Oswego River)
2. Mouth of Oneida to village of Phoenix

Length 11.5 mi (without detours; at least twice as long if every detour is taken)

Drop Negligible

Difficulty Class I

Problems Heavy boat traffic in canal section May 1 to Oct 15, when canal is open to traffic; turbulence at put-in and crosscurrents at takeout if water is high and gates are open

Maps Central Square, Brewerton, Baldwinsville; DeLorme p 75

Contributor Daniel Geist

Launch Access is below Caughdenoy Dam. This is reached by taking I-81 N or S to Rt 49 Exit N of Oneida Lake. Travel W on 49 to County Rt 12, W on 12 to dam. The launch is rocky if water is high. This is a popular fishing spot, and there is plenty of parking both above and below the dam.

Description This trip is most pleasant in spring or fall when the Barge Canal is not open; 9 mi of the route is along the canalized part of the river. There is a nice mix of wooded rural scenery and year-round and summer homes. Paddling is simple and straightforward for the most part, except as noted.

Caughdenoy Dam to Three Rivers: The trip begins in a loop of the Oneida River, off the canal. After approximately 2.5 mi the canal enters L, but at several other places the canoeist may also paddle the original course of the river. The first of these, about 1 mi farther, is the Glosky Island Channel, which deviates S from the canal for 1.5 mi. In another mile or so, it is possible to detour L around Schroeppel Island. Shortly thereafter, Mud Creek, which drains Clay Marsh, enters from the south. Depending on down trees and water level, this can be navigated upstream for several miles.

Just beyond the mouth of Mud Creek, the route passes under Oak Orchard Bridge; just E of here one wall of the Oak Orchard Lock, which dates from the 1837 Oneida River improvement, may be seen. About 1.5 mi farther, Horseshoe Island Channel deviates from the canal to the N. This detour is about 4.5 mi long; at its north end, the canoeist can enter Peter Scott Swamp via either Fish Creek or Sixmile Creek. The main canal, here called the Big Bend Cut, takes slightly more than 1 mi to reach the west end of Horseshoe Island Channel.

About .2 mi farther, the Rt 481 bridge is reached. There is a state boat launch site here. Between this point and the mouth of the Oneida, the Bonstead's Island Channel to the N offers a short detour. Shortly beyond this point, the route enters the Oswego River.

Three Rivers to Phoenix: The Oswego River is canoeable for its entire length. However, it is also canalized for its entire length. At the numerous locks there are dams and powerhouse intakes, which may or may not create dangerous currents, depending on whether or not the gates are open. The canoeist will also encounter large and small powerboats. For these reasons, the trip may be more pleasant in early spring or late fall, although there are always interesting side channels to explore where these conditions will not be encountered. Rts 57 and 48 roughly parallel the river, one on each side, making access convenient at many points.

About 2 mi downstream from Three Rivers (the confluence of the Seneca and the Oneida to form the Oswego), the preferred canoe route departs from the canal and passes E of Stowell or Treasure Island. To avoid the swift current and turbulence above the dam, the paddler should hug the east shore as he approaches Phoenix.

Takeout Just below Stowell Island, access is possible at Henley Park, Lock St, in Phoenix. There can be crosscurrents here if dam is open and water is high.

Jamesville Reservoir; Butternut Creek

County: Onondaga

Segment ↕ All

Length ↔ 4 mi (round trip)

Drop ↘ Negligible

Difficulty ① Class I

Problems ✻ Usually cold and windy in November; wind surfers in summer

Maps Jamesville; DeLorme p 61

Contributor Byron L. Craft

Launch Take Rt 173, from its intersection with Rt 11 in Syracuse, E 4 mi to Jamesville. Just before crossing the bridge, turn S on Apulia Rd 2 mi to Jamesville Beach County Park. Park here and carry to the area just right of the beach for an easy launch.

Description Jamesville Reservoir, like most lakes, can be difficult when windy. Avoid the dam at the north end. Butternut Creek, which enters the lake through a marshy area at the south end, is quite interesting and attractive and contains large numbers of ducks. The stream channel through the marsh is readily apparent. About .25 mi up the creek from the launch point is a blowdown which may be difficult to get around. From this point, it is a pleasant paddle of about .75 mi to the footbridge. The current picks up in this stretch, and progress upstream depends on the skill and ambition of the paddler. At this writing (1991) the footbridge has collapsed on one side and blocks further passage. It is probably not worth the trouble to attempt to get around this obstacle.

Takeout As with most lake trips, takeout is at the launch point.

Otisco Lake

County: Onondaga

Segment Entire lake

Length 12 mi (round trip)

Drop Zero

Difficulty Class I

Problems Usual lake problems with wind

Maps Marcellus, Spafford, Otisco Valley; DeLorme p 61

Contributor Robert J. Gang, Jr.

Launch There are several convenient access points: on the east side near the dam, which is at the north end of the lake; at the Amber Marina; near the causeway on the east side; and at the causeway on the west side. The parking at the dam is limited, and a fee is charged to launch at the marina. To reach the village of Amber, turn S off Rt 20, SW of Syracuse, onto Amber Rd. Thence the Otisco Valley Rd leads S along the east shore to the causeway, which crosses the lake about 1 mile N of the south end. The old bridge at the causeway has been out since the 1940s.

Description This is a typical "finger" lake, albeit a small one, formed when the glacier carved the steep-sided valley of a south-flowing stream into the characteristic U-shape of a glacial valley. At the same time, the land to the north was lowered, and as the glacier receded it left a terminal moraine at the north, damming the water into a lake. Eventually, Ninemile Creek cut a small path through the moraine to become the outlet of Otisco Lake. Ninemile Creek is generally regarded as not canoeable.

This is a delightful lake to paddle. The west shore rises steeply and is covered with forest reminiscent of the Adirondacks. On the east shore, lake cottages and camps are backed by rolling farm land. The west shore also has seasonal homes and camps, as well as a restaurant which offers docking privileges. Canoeists may also visit the village of Amber, which has a hardware store, a small grocery, and a tavern.

Spafford Creek enters the lake at the south end through a marsh containing ducks, geese, beaver, and a few loons. Fishing is good here and in the main lake for bass, norlunge, and walleye, as well as other species.

Caution ✖ On any of the Finger Lakes, moderate S or N winds can build surprisingly large waves at the leeward end of the lake, and the lake has a way of channeling winds from other directions so that they appear to be either N or S.

Takeout At any of the launch points.

Owasco Outlet

County: Cayuga

Segment ↕ Throopsville to Seneca River (Mosquito Point)

Length ↔ 8 mi

Drop ↘ 100 ft

Difficulty ① Class I

Problems ✻ Upper part: easy rapids, shoals, log-ends protruding from bridge supports

Maps Auburn, Weedsport, Montezuma; DeLorme pp 60, 74

Contributor Alice Broberg

Launch To reach the recommended access point, take Rt 38 N from Auburn or S from Port Byron. Turn W on Turnpike Rd at Sunoco Bread and Butter Store. Drive .6 mi to bridge and park on R at east end of narrow bridge rail on downstream side. The other three "corners" of the bridge are posted. Carry 50 ft to a grassy, level site and launch in narrow eddy. There is room for only one car here; shuttle other vehicles to takeout point.

Description Owasco Outlet flows from Owasco Lake to the Seneca River, passing through the heart of Auburn. To the unwary canoeist, a woodsy trail in that city leading to a spot just below a dam spillway might seem to constitute an ideal launch opportunity. No signs are there to warn that the stream drops from the 711-ft lake level to 540 at a gaging station in 4 mi of falls, dams, log jams, and gorges. *NO* launch point upstream from the one described above is recommended by this guide.

The trip from Throopsville to Mosquito Point is pleasant, with just enough current and impediments to make it interesting. From the launch point to Port Byron, canoeing is not feasible at less than M water levels; however, the lower part can be run from spring through fall. Once launched, the canoeist should be prepared to backpaddle and avoid log-ends, but long stretches have no impediments. There are a few riffles and some shoals to be skirted; a set of rapids can be bypassed in an easier channel if desired. The shoreline consists of wooded hillsides, becoming steeper as Port Byron is approached.

About 5 mi after launch, paddlers arrive at the Rts 31/38 bridge in Port Byron. This makes a good lunch stop or intermediate takeout point. A gravel beach with space for six canoes has a 15-ft gravel path leading up to Rochester and Church streets and a grassy park 3 blocks W of the center of town. There is space to park two cars at the bridge, and other parking nearby.

Leaving the lunch stop, the route passes under the I-90 bridge after .5 mi. A strong current makes the remaining 3 mi to the barge canal a short trip, and those who continue are rewarded with forest scenery and waterfowl, including, if they're lucky, ducklings and Canada goslings. The stream is also a spawning site for walleyed pike.

Takeout As the Seneca River/NY State Barge Canal is reached, the route turns slightly L and across the canal to the takeout at Mosquito Point on Haiti Island. (See p 210 for a complete description of this access point.)

Note ☞ An oil spill at Port Byron in early 1991 caused environmental damage, the total extent and duration of which is unknown at this writing. An observer in April 1991 reported that there were no obvious indications of the spill.

Seneca River (Seneca and Cayuga Canals)

Counties: Seneca, Cayuga

Segment ↕ Seneca Park to Rt 31

Length ↔ 18 mi

Drop ↘ 70 ft, almost all at locks

Difficulty ① Class I

Problems ✻ None

Maps Geneva S, Geneva N, Seneca Falls, Cayuga, Montezuma; DeLorme pp 59, 60, 74

Contributors Ron Canter, Daniel Geist

Launch This trip begins at a state launch site on the north side of the Seneca River at Seneca Lake State Park, which is about 2 mi E of Geneva on US 20. There is no camping at the park. Geneva is on Rt 14, 6 mi S of its interchange with I-90.

Description Although this is entirely a flatwater trip on a commercial canal and some parts are dull or commercially developed, long stretches are rural and attractive. Lockkeepers are uniformly friendly and helpful.

From the north end of Seneca Lake, the canalized Seneca River flows E 12 mi to the northern tip of Cayuga Lake. About 1.5 mi from launch another state access site is passed L. The shores are lined with buildings through Waterloo, at the 4.5-mi point, where Lock 4 begins the 60-ft descent to the Cayuga Lake level. The falls at Seneca Falls, 3 mi farther, are drowned under Van Cleef Lake, which was created by the dam at Locks 2 and 3.

A canoeist describes his experience on this route: "Riding through the locks in a canoe is quite an experience, for the drop in each is over 20 feet. As you paddle in, you are looking over the rim. A few minutes later you are at the bottom of a deep box looking up. (The lockkeeper was happy to lock us through and show off his toy. We were suitably impressed.)"

Below the locks the river runs with some current through a wooded ravine for 2 mi, then opens into marshes for 1 mi to the northern tip of Cayuga Lake. Here it turns N through Lock 1 into the Montezuma Marshes. While the Montezuma National Wildlife Refuge may be a birdwatcher's paradise, the route through it is dull for a canoeist. The river is channelized, the land is flat, and dikes hide the marsh from view.

After passing under I-90 16 mi from launch, the Cayuga and Seneca Canal joins the canalized Clyde River, the modern Erie Canal. About 1 mi from the junction, the route crosses the course of the Old Erie Canal, with the ruins of an aqueduct on the right. One mile farther the Rt 31 bridge is reached.

Takeout The access point is under the west end of the Rt 31 bridge. This point is reached by taking I-90 to the Weedsport Exit, thence traveling S on Rt 34 .5 mi to Rt 31, then about 9 mi W on 31. A dirt road at the northwest end of the bridge approach leads to the river bank. At one time there was a state buoy boat house and a wooden dock here; nothing but piling remains now. There is plenty of parking under the bridge and along the dirt road.

Camping Cayuga Lake State Park, 3 mi E of Seneca Falls, offers camping; there are also several commercial campgrounds in the general area.

Seneca River

Counties: Cayuga, Wayne, Seneca

Segment Rt 31 to Mosquito Pt

Length 10 mi

Drop Negligible

Difficulty Class I

Problems Short carry at RR tracks

Maps Montezuma; DeLorme p 74

Contributor Daniel Geist

Launch Access is under the west end of the Rt 31 bridge. (See previous entry.)

Description Although the very beginning and the very end of this trip are in the canalized part of the river, about nine-tenths of it is in the loop of the river which departs from the Barge Canal and flows around the Howland Island Wildlife Management Area. One canoeist describes the trip as "a birdwatcher's dream."

Traveling N from the launch point, after about 1.5 mi, the route reaches, at Marker 524, the second of two side channels on the L. This is where the river leaves the canal. The abandoned rights-of-way of the West Shore RR and the Rochester and Eastern trolley line cross the river, as do the present Conrail tracks. At the Conrail crossing, a short carry over an access road is necessary before paddling under the tracks. About .8 mi past this, a side channel R returns to the Barge Canal, but the more attractive route continues in the river.

From here on, the river makes a gradual bend, ultimately heading S. At about the 9-mi point, a sort of T-intersection is reached. Here the waterway goes both SE and SW to rejoin the canal, forming Haiti Island. The route goes SE to the canal, then makes a sharp right. After about .25 mi, the takeout is reached.

Takeout This is a Barge Canal mooring area with a parking lot and tie-ups for barges. It is reached by car from the Rt 38 bridge over the canal at Mosquito Pt. The sharp turn from the bridge W onto the Haiti Island Rd is easy to miss.

Clyde River

Counties: Wayne, Seneca

Segment ↕ Lock 26 to Mays Point

Length ↔ 8.5 mi

Drop ↘ Negligible

Difficulty ① Class I

Problems ✻ The one portage required is muddy at low water

Maps Savannah, Seneca Falls; DeLorme pp 73, 59

Contributor Byron L. Craft

Launch Access is at Lock 26, S of the town of Clyde. Turn L off Rt 414 onto Redfield St, which becomes Glover Rd. After about 1.5 mi, turn L on Lock Rd and follow for 1 mi to the end. Park by the lock tender's building. Launch should be upstream from the lock, since the bank downstream is very rocky. Launch in a small dip W of the lock after arranging with the lock tender to lock through.

Description The Clyde now consists of a series of four loops off the Erie Barge Canal. These loops, the original stream bed, are all SW of the canal. The first loop is blocked by a low bridge which requires a short, muddy portage. The best part of the trip is immediately thereafter. In summer, orioles nest in the tall willows, and a lucky paddler may see an otter. The second and third loops, while pleasant, may be blocked by timber washed in by the spring floods. The fourth loop borders the Montezuma National Wildlife Refuge. Watch for a hole in the embankment, through which a glimpse of the refuge may be obtained.

Takeout Access is easily feasible at Mays Point, under the Rt 89 bridge, just S of Lock 25. (At this point, the canoeist is not on the canal proper, but on the fourth loop.) Parking is available nearby. Unless it has been corrected recently, the USGS Seneca Falls quadrant calls the highway Rt 414 at this point, but it isn't; it's Rt 89. Rt 89 roughly parallels Cayuga Lake, to the W.

Notes Since there is little or no gradient, this trip may be run in either direction. If it is run from Mays Point to Lock 26, however, arranging with the lock tender and getting out may be more difficult.

Locks officially close for the season in November and open again in May; water level is lowered during the winter.

Camping Oak Orchard Marina and Campground, mailing address Savannah, is in the vicinity of Mays Point. It is a public commercial campground.

Lamoka Lake/ Waneta Lake

Counties: Steuben, Schuyler

Segment Bradford to Wayne

Length 8 mi

Drop Negligible

Difficulty Class I

Problems None, except for some tough carries if the trip continues past Wayne

Maps Bradford, Wayne; DeLorme p 45

Contributor Ron Canter

Launch The best launch point is about .33 mi N of Bradford at a landing with good parking on the west shore of Mill Pond. A less attractive launch point is at the dam, which raises the level of Mud Creek and Mill Pond to 1099 ft above sea level, the level of Lakes Waneta and Lamoka. The dam is about .2 mi E of Bradford on an unnamed road. Bradford is reached by taking Rt 17 NW from Corning or SE from Bath to Savona, then turning NE onto Rt 226. After about 8 mi, either of two left turns onto roads which are not named on the USGS quadrants lead to Bradford.

Description This is one segment of a very interesting and scenic horseshoe trip from Bradford to Hammondsport. The entire trip, with carries, would make a very long day; unfortunately, there is no state campsite directly along the route. There is a commercial public campsite, Lakeview, mailing address Dundee, on Keuka Lake just north of Alexander Landing. Probably the best solution for those in less than perfect trim is to spot a vehicle at Wayne.

The route begins in Mill Pond, a pretty little body of water 1 mi long, tucked under Whitehead Hill. The connection to Lamoka Lake is via Mud Creek, which is prettier and wider (since the dam construction) than the name would imply and has some cottages along its shores. In the opinion of the contributor, Lamoka Lake is the most attractive part of the route. Its 1.5-mi length has a nice balance between wild and developed shores, and the land sweeps up to high hills on every side. Near the north end, a small island, Red Bank, is undeveloped and unposted at this writing.

The outlet to Waneta Lake is a narrow swamp channel E of a house at the northwest corner of Lamoka. It is a pretty run through marsh and meadow, about .75 mi long. At the halfway point, it is bridged by the road from Tyrone to practically nowhere, and there is a state boat launch site here.

Canoes, but not motorboats, can pass through the culvert under this bridge. At about this point, between the lakes, there was once a Native American village which dated back 3000 years or more. The location of the village is not surprising, since it straddled a transportation route between the St. Lawrence and Susquehanna watersheds at its highest point. Waneta Lake is 3 mi long, and cottages line its straight shores. Unless there is a very strong north wind, traversing its length offers no particular problems or high interest. There is a narrow man-made canalized outlet at the north end, which can be found by aiming L of the church steeple in Wayne.

Takeout Takeout is possible but steep at the first road, 1000 ft along the channel described above. There is no canoeable culvert here; the canal passes under the road via a small pipe. This local road travels due S out of Wayne to the lake. Boats must be dragged up the short steep trail R to the road. There is room for several cars here.

Special Note To make the entire trip to Hammondsport from the pipe and road described above, carry 700 ft on the right bank past a second road and culvert. Slide down a steep, rocky bank and relaunch. At Rt 230 take out R by a cemetery and carry over the canal. Immediately turn R on Keuka Hill Rd. Carry just over a mile downhill and turn R on Rt 54. After .25 mi, turn L and carry 400 ft down to Keuka Lake at Alexander Landing, near the village of Keuka, where a public boat ramp is squeezed between cottages. Those using the ramp must offload and park a few blocks away. Total carry is 1.5 mi, all downhill on good roads. Keuka is reached via Rt 54 S from Penn Yan. (See map, p 217.)

Keuka Lake

Counties: Steuben, Schuyler

Segment Alexander Landing (Village of Keuka) to Hammondsport

Length 8.5 mi

Drop Negligible

Difficulty Class I

Problems Serious waves when windy

Maps Wayne, Hammondsport; DeLorme pp 44, 45

Contributor Ron Canter

Launch There are plenty of points of access to Keuka Lake, including state boat launch sites near Hammondsport at the south end, Penn Yan at the northeast, and at Keuka Lake State Park at the northwest end. However, this particular trip begins at Alexander Landing, near the village of Keuka. (For details on the launch site, see p 214.)

Description Keuka Lake is the only Finger Lake to be forked; Keuka means approximately that in the Algonquin tongue. It divides at an impressive peak called Bluff Point, which rises steeply about 700 ft above the water. The northwest arm is 6.5 mi long, the northeast, 11, the south, 7. All of the lake is eminently canoeable, subject to the usual annoyances of wind and motorboats. The shores, fairly steep for the most part, are lined with summer cottages. This is also one of the centers of the New York State wine industry and there are many vineyards here, including the renowned Bully Hill. Most wineries offer tours and free samples.

The trip to Hammondsport will be uneventful on most days if the canoeist begins early enough to reach his destination before the wind gets up. If it is very windy, the trip ranges from frightening to impossible. Normally, the route hugs the east shore from Keuka to Hammondsport; however, if prevailing westerlies are anticipated, it is feasible to paddle approximately .5 mi across the lake to the protection of the west shore. Unfortunately, on all the Finger Lakes, west winds have a way of twisting around to blow from whatever direction the paddler is headed toward.

Note ☞ Prevailing southwesterlies in summer might make it more practical to do this trip in reverse order, from Hammondsport to Alexander Landing, or to canoe just from Hammondsport to the state park.

Takeout There are several possible takeout points, including two state boat ramps, in Hammondsport. One of these is at the R of the inlet. Hammondsport is reached by car by traveling US 15 in either direction to Bath, then turning NE on Rt 54.

This trip, combined with the preceding one, takes the canoeist from the Susquehanna to the St. Lawrence watershed. It is easier for us today than it was for the Iroquois, who had several such routes, some of them involving carries of 10 miles or more, because engineers changed the normal flow of Waneta/Lamoka lakes from south to north in order to provide a sufficient head of water to a power plant.

It would be theoretically possible for a hardy band of fit canoeists to travel from Montreal to Norfolk via this route or between any two-way points. From Ithaca, for example, they might paddle Cayuga Lake and the Cayuga and Seneca Canal to Seneca Lake. Landing at Dresden, the canoeists would carry up .67 mi to the Keuka Outlet takeout described on p 221. After lining, poling, and wading up to Cascade

Canoe Route from Seneca Lake to Cohocton River

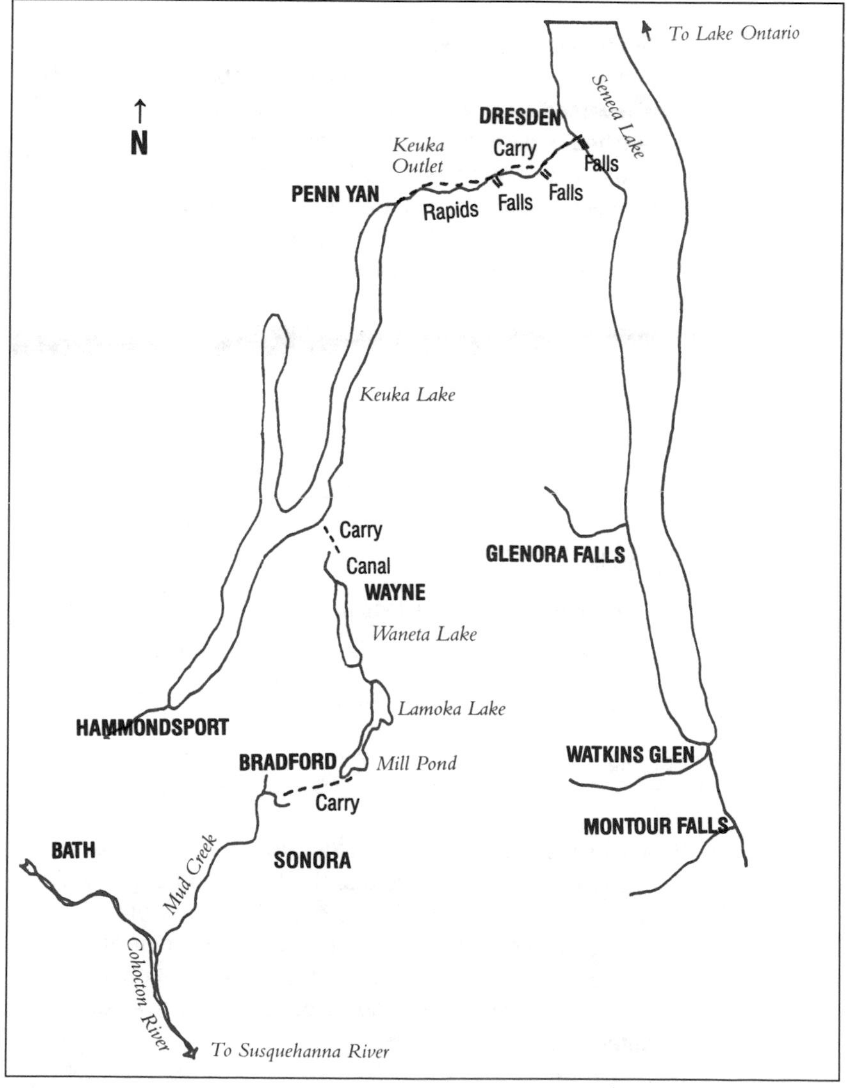

Mills, there would be a 4.5-mi uphill carry to Penn Yan, where boats could be launched into Keuka Lake and paddled to Keuka. Thence, the trip described on pp 212–214 is reversed, with some more uphill carrying, until Bradford is reached. A carry of about 2.67 mi takes the group to Birdsaw Hollow, where Mud Creek becomes canoeable thanks to a low gradient and the work of beavers. From here, it's all downhill to Chesapeake Bay.

Keuka Lake Outlet

County: Yates

Segment ↕ Keuka Lake to Rt 14

Length ↔ 7 mi

Drop ↘ 255 ft

Difficulty ② Class II, occasionally Class III

Problems ✻ Rapids, waterfalls, down trees, short steep downhill carries

Maps Penn Yan, Dresden; DeLorme p 59

Contributor Ron Canter

Launch Access is easy at the Penn Yan town park that is on the west shore of the lake at the beginning of the outlet. The park is in the southwest part of town, W of Rt 54. There is also a park and boat ramp L, .67 mi further along the route from Keuka Lake, which makes a good alternate launch point. Plenty of parking is available at either park.

Description Keuka Lake is 715 ft above sea level; Seneca Lake, 445. Keuka Outlet covers this drop in about 8 mi. While with a few exceptions the gradient is remarkably even, making it a Class I-II sluice, there are some stretches which are more difficult and some which are impossible.

Water level: Rises and falls are slower and more modest than in a similar but non-lakefed stream. It takes a great deal of rain to raise the level of the lake, but once it is up, the outlet level will remain high for days. A fine hiking trail, the Outlet Trail, formerly a RR grade, parallels the stream, L, for the entire distance.

After leaving the recommended launch point, when the stream expands to a marshy pond, the route hugs the south bank. The scenery here consists mostly of litter. Soon the second possible access point is passed. About 800 ft after the route passes under a bridge, flatwater ends at an old dam with gated sluices on each side. Land on the grassy center. The shorter carry is to lift over and lower the boats straight down to the water; this is direct but awkward. Longer but easier is to carry to the R, go under the Rt 54 bridge, and relaunch downstream.

The water level for the entire trip will be accurately predicted by the water level under the footbridge here. The next mile is very fast and winding between steep banks and consists of Class I and II rapids. Beware of down timber and log jams. A Class II rock garden precedes the bridge at Keuka Mills. In this first mile, there was once a series of mills and dams; only traces remain.

The next .75 mi, to the ruins of Milo Mills, is more of the same until near the end. Here the stream makes a sharp right turn through the remains of the old dam, 500 ft above the mill. This is a Class III rapids and must be scouted; it is often blocked by debris which cannot be seen from above the bend. Portage is possible on the left.

Caution ✖ For the next 1.25 mi, the stream travels through a pretty, narrow valley. When it starts winding through a marsh, WAKE UP! Take out where the stream slows against a hillock on the left. Visible ahead on the horizon is the old dam at Seneca Mills, with a break in the middle. This is the first step in a three-step falls which is totally unrunnable. The falls and mill foundations are squeezed between high bluffs in a very scenic fashion. Carry along the Outlet Trail, L, past the falls and stone ruins. Turn R through brick ruins. Slide boats down to a fallen brick pillar in the stream, near an eddy which is small but adequate for relaunching.

Next the stream scoots through a shale gorge, then winds down a shut-in valley past the bridge at Mays Mills. About .4 mi below Mays Mills, Outlet Tire can be seen ahead L.

Extreme Caution ✖ Take out here L. *Don't* continue down enticing Class II rapids below shale cliffs. Around the bend is a 25-ft waterfall between a rock wall on the right and the concrete walls of the abandoned Cascade Mills on the left.

Carry 500 ft through the Outlet Tire parking lot, then L around the old factory to a launch point below the falls. The ditch between Outlet Tire and the trail is the bed of the long-abandoned Seneca and Keuka Canal. Below the carry are two tricky Class II rapids under a shale cliff with a band of sandstone sandwiched in.

For the next 1.75 mi to Rt 14, Keuka Outlet is swift but flat, in an isolated valley. The stream is occasionally blocked by fallen trees. Next, the route passes under the high bridge of Rt 14.

Extreme Caution ✖ Take out L 500 ft below this bridge, where the stream turns R. Five hundred feet below this takeout the stream is swallowed by a tunnel under the RR causeway, with a 10-ft falls at the far portal. Don't get caught in this trap.

Takeout As indicated above, boats must be taken out 500 ft below the Rt 14 bridge. The takeout is reached by car via Rt 54 E from Penn Yan to Rt 14, continuing straight ahead .1 mi when 54 ends at 14. Carry and drag boats100 ft. N to the Outlet Trail, then carry 200 ft E to a parking area at the end of the trail next to the RR tracks. Now go have a good lunch; you've earned it.

West River

County: Ontario

Segment From bridge to Canandaigua Lake, also upstream from bridge (see text)

Length 8 mi

Drop Negligible

Difficulty Class I

Problems Waves on lake, beaver dams

Maps Middlesex; DeLorme p 58

Contributor Daan Zwick

Launch The recommended access point is at a state boat launch site 4 mi N of Naples off County Rt 21, at bridge. Parking is readily available here. Naples, the home of Widmer's winery, is reached via Rt 21 from Canandaigua, a distance of about 20 mi. Other access points are described below.

Description West River is a small stream which empties into Canandaigua Lake at the south end. From the launch point downstream it is flatwater, wandering through a marsh which makes up part of the High Tor Wildlife Management Area. The 4 mi upstream from the bridge constitute slowly moving water in marsh and swampy woods. The attractions of the stream include its relative remoteness and extensive wildlife.

Upstream, the route very soon reaches an abandoned RR bridge and a broken beaver dam, each of which requires careful maneuvering or a very short portage. These obstacles effectively prevent motorboats from traveling beyond this spot; above this point, the canoeist shares the stream only with wildlife. The next mile is a wide marsh, which then narrows to a smaller stream with noticeable current. At H water, it is possible to explore some distance away from the main channel into the woods. Farther up there are several beaver dams in succession; at each one the canoeist may decide to persevere or turn back, but they are fairly easily dragged over. Although the stream usually has enough water for navigation throughout the year, in midsummer a profusion of duckweed may be found in this upper part of the trip, making it less pleasant but not impossible. This thins out as the canoeist proceeds upstream to the more wooded swamp, for the current and shade discourage its growth. The main channel can be identified by the presence of current and the beaver dams.

Downstream from the launch point, after about 1 mi, another access point is passed, L. From here it is about 3 mi to the lake. The conditions and wildlife are similar to those encountered above the launch point, except that of course the stream is wider and deeper and readily accessible to motorboats. Caution should be exercised approaching the river mouth; a strong northerly wind can kick up quite astonishing waves at this end of the lake.

West River

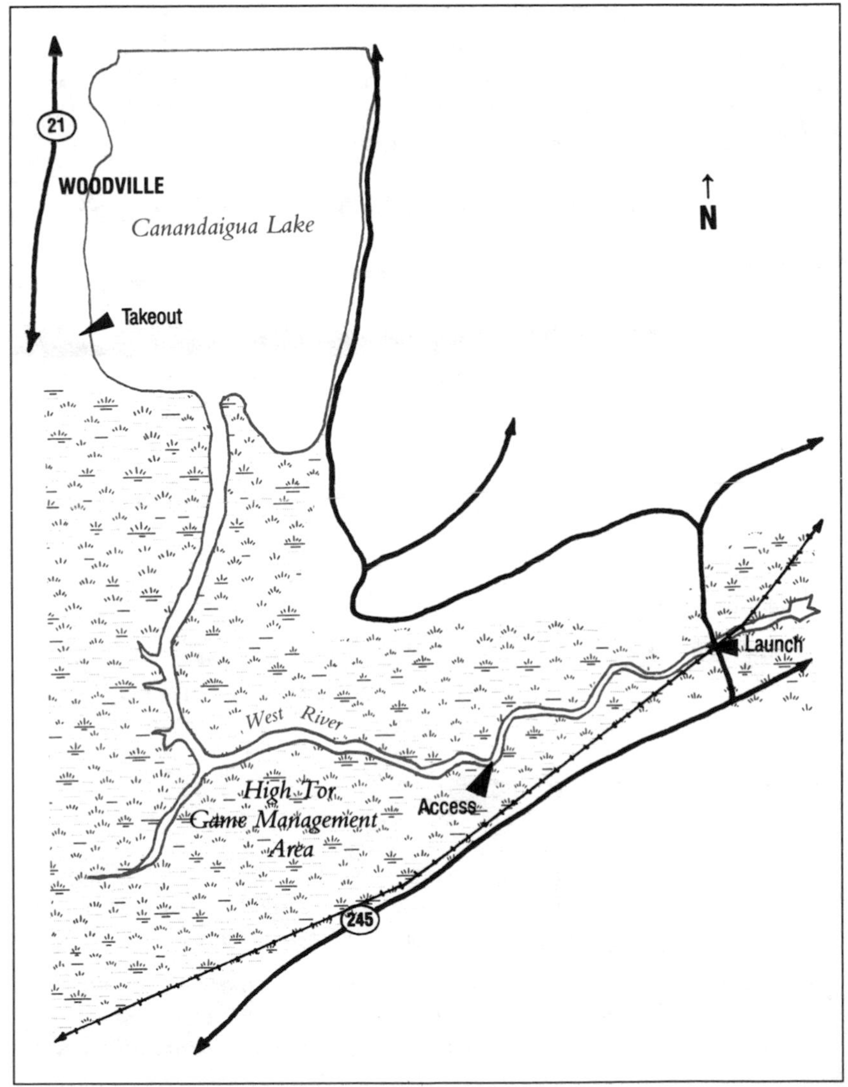
21
WOODVILLE
Canandaigua Lake
N
Takeout
West River
High Tor
Game Management
Area
Access
Launch
245

Takeout The state boat launch site on Canandaigua Lake at Woodville is a good takeout point in calm weather. This site has toilet facilities and adequate parking. It is, however, .5 mi across the south end of the lake from the mouth of the West River, and when the wind is blowing, the canoeist may very well decide to return to the launch point. Current does not prevent this trip from being run from one access point to another access point or as a round trip.

Canandaigua Outlet

Counties: Ontario, Wayne

Segment Manchester to Lyons

Length 25 mi

Drop 165 ft

Difficulty Class I

Problems Debris, an old broken dam

Maps Clifton Springs, Phelps, Geneva N, Lyons, Newark; DeLorme pp 58, 59, 73

Contributors Alice Broberg, Daniel Geist

Launch The Rt 96 bridge in Manchester is a popular launch point. There is limited space to park just off the road. This is less than a mile S of the I-90 Rt 21 interchange.

Description Canandaigua Outlet may be unique among New York streams in that it not only parallels the Thomas E. Dewey Thruway (I-90) for much of its length but at one point flows for some distance between the eastbound and westbound lanes; paddlers can hear cars whizzing past them on both sides. In spite of this, most of this trip is remote and wooded, with wildflowers and birds, including wood ducks, in addition to tall old trees. Fishing for smallmouth bass is said to be good.

Although an annual race is held from Shortsville to Manchester, in recent years there has seldom been enough water to canoe from the lake to Manchester at any other time, two releases from the dam being necessary to provide sufficient water for the race. Canoeists usually put in at the above launch point for a scenic trip which follows the Thruway for 13 highway miles, then turns N 8 mi more before emptying into the Barge Canal at Lyons. The 25 or more river miles is a bit long for a day trip, but there are many intermediate access points.

At MH or H levels the stream moves along briskly from the launch point, and the paddler must do some maneuvering in shallow areas and around debris. After .5 mi, the stream passes under the eastbound lane of I-90, then turns to flow E between the two lanes for 2 mi, after which it turns N to pass under the other lane. Six miles from launch near Clifton Springs is a graveled boat launch site with ample parking off Rt 96 next to the Cty Rt 25 bridge. Known as Outlet Rd, Cty 25 hugs the north side of Canandaigua Outlet as it makes a leisurely northerly loop for the next 6 mi, passing several abandoned bridges and possible access sites. For the most part it seems remote and wild in spite of nearby homes. At this writing, debris in the stream requires dodging from time to time; a popular access point near Phelps where Rt 88 crosses is not usable for this reason.

One mi from the Rt 88 bridge, the stream turns SE and passes under I-90 again, flowing through the north side of

Phelps. After about another mile, Flint Creek enters R at the N. Wayne St bridge. Another good access point, with room to park, is here; a path on the NE side of the bridge leads to the stream. The river swings between I-90 and Rt 96 until Pre-emption Rd bridge (another good access point), 2.5 mi from Flint Creek, where it begins a gradual turn N, flowing under I-90 for the last time 1.25 mi farther. From this point, Rt 14 parallels the outlet to the east.

The moderately strong current moves N around islands and shoals, which also catch debris to be avoided. Several islands and alternative channels are 1 mi N of I-90; a commercial campground is just E here. Next come riffles and shallows, then deep water through a broken dam to add excitement just before the bridge at Alloway. An access point is L just before the bridge. Many paddlers choose to end the trip here, as the takeout is more comfortable than that listed below. Three more miles of good paddling takes the canoeist the rest of the way to Lyons.

Takeout About 100 yds short of the junction with the Barge Canal, access is possible L. It is not an easy exit, involving fast current and a steep muddy bank. It is reached by car by turning S off Rt 31 onto Leach Rd, across the canal from Lyons. Parking is possible on a small dirt road, a spur off Leach.

Caution Paddlers *must* take out here if they wish to avoid going over the 6-ft dam just below this point.

Camping Cheerful Valley (commercial) Campground in Phelps is very near Canandaigua Outlet just N of the last I-90 bridge.

Ganargua Creek

County: Wayne

Segment ↕ Rt 88 to Abbey Park on Lyons Rd

Length ↔ 8 mi

Drop ↘ 30 ft

Difficulty ① Class I

Problems ✻ Downed trees, log jams, one or more chutes under bridges

Maps Newark; DeLorme p 73

Contributor Ron Schlie

Launch Recommended launch point is at the Rt 88 bridge about 2 mi N of the town of Newark. This access necessitates parking at the side of a busy highway. There are a number of other possible access points along Ganargua Creek, both during this stretch and above, toward Palmyra. Some are intended primarily for trailered powerboats; some charge a fee.

Description The nature of this stream was changed with the construction of the Barge Canal. Water flows out of the canal into the creek, as well as vice versa. The bad news is that this makes Ganargua Creek quite murky. The good news is that it makes it canoeable when the water level is too low for boating in other streams in the area. While this is not life-threatening white water, the current moves right along, and the possibility of obstructions requires the paddler to keep his wits about him. Beginners should not attempt this trip except in the company of more experienced paddlers.

The first section, from the launch point to Mud Mills Rd, passes under a RR bridge about a half mile from the start. About 1 mi farther, under the Mud Mills Rd bridge, there is a chute which is runnable; newcomers should scout it. Especially at high water, it may be desirable to line down.

There is a steadily moving current between Mud Mills Rd and Narsen Bridge Park and the stream is blocked in several places, requiring tight paddle work or short carries. Narsen Bridge Park, which has toilets and picnic tables, makes a good lunch stop. The current slows from Narsen Bridge Park to Abbey Park, and more homes and camps appear. When there is an east wind on this stretch, paddling is difficult; otherwise the section presents no problems.

Takeout Recommended takeout is at Abbey Park, which is on Lyons Rd (as is so often the case, this is called Lyons Rd in Newark and Newark Rd in Lyons) about .5 mi W of Lyons. Located where the Barge Canal and Ganargua Creek meet, the park has toilet facilities, picnic tables, and a covered pavilion in addition to the boat launch.

Index

Notes

Notes

Notes

Notes

Notes

Notes

Notes

Notes

Other Publications
of
The Adirondack Mountain Club, Inc.
RR 3, Box 3055
Lake George, N.Y. 12845-9522
(518) 668-4447

BOOKS

Adirondack Canoe Waters: North Flow
Adirondack Canoe Waters: South & West Flow
85 Acres: A Field Guide to the Adirondack Alpine Summits
Classic Adirondack Ski Tours
Winterwise: A Backpacker's Guide
Climbing in the Adirondacks
Guide to Adirondack Trails: High Peaks Region
Guide to Adirondack Trails: Northern Region
Guide to Adirondack Trails: Central Region
Guide to Adirondack Trails: Northville-Placid Trail
Guide to Adironadack Trails: West-Central Region
Guide to Adirondack Trails: Eastern Region
Guide to Adirondack Trails: Southern Region
Guide to Catskill Trails
An Adirondack Sampler, Day Hikes for All Seasons
An Adirondack Sampler II, Backpacking Trips
Geology of the Adirondack High Peaks Region
The Adirondack Reader
Adirondack Pilgrimage
Our Wilderness: How the People of New York Found, Changed, and Preserved the Adirondacks
Adirondack Wildguide (distributed by ADK)

MAPS

Trails of the Adirondack High Peaks Region
Trails of the Northern Region
Trails of the Central Region
Northville-Placid Trail
Trails of the West-Central Region
Trails of the Eastern Region
Trails of the Southern Region

Price list available on request.